PROCESS THEOLOGY:
A GUIDE FOR THE PERPLEXED

T&T Clark *Guides for the Perplexed*

T&T Clark's *Guides for the Perplexed* are clear, concise and accessible introductions to thinkers, writers, and subjects that students and readers can find especially challenging. Concentrating specifically on what it is that makes the subject difficult to grasp, these books explain and explore key themes and ideas, guiding the reader towards a thorough understanding of demanding material.

Guides for the Perplexed available from T&T Clark:

De Lubac: A Guide for the Perplexed, David Grumett
Christian Bioethics: A Guide for the Perplexed, Agneta Sutton
Calvin: A Guide for the Perplexed, Paul Helm
Tillich: A Guide for the Perplexed, Andrew O'Neill
The Trinity: A Guide for the Perplexed, Paul M. Collins
Christology: A Guide for the Perplexed, Alan Spence
Wesley: A Guide for the Perplexed, Jason E. Vickers
Pannenberg: A Guide for the Perplexed, Timothy Bradshaw
Balthasar: A Guide for the Perplexed, Rodney Howsare
Theological Anthropology: A Guide for the Perplexed, Marc Cortez
Benedict XVI: A Guide for the Perplexed, Tracey Rowland
Eucharist: A Guide for the Perplexed, Ralph N. McMichael

Forthcoming Titles:

Political Theology: A Guide for the Perplexed, Elizabeth Philips
Martyrdom: A Guide for the Perplexed, Middleton
Sin: A Guide for the Perplexed, Derek Nelson

PROCESS THEOLOGY: A GUIDE FOR THE PERPLEXED

BRUCE G. EPPERLY

B L O O M S B U R Y

LONDON · NEW DELHI · NEW YORK · SYDNEY

Bloomsbury T&T Clark

An imprint of Bloomsbury Publishing Plc

50 Bedford Square	175 Fifth Avenue
London	New York
WC1B 3DP	NY 10010
UK	USA

www.bloomsbury.com

First published 2011
Reprinted 2011, 2012, 2013

British Library Cataloguing-in-Publication Data
A catalogue record for this book is available from the British Library.

ISBN: HB: 978-0-567-63255-5
PB: 978-0-567-59669-7

Library of Congress Cataloging-in-Publication Data
A catalog record for this book is available from the Library of Congress.

Typeset by Newgen Imaging Systems Pvt Ltd, Chennai, India
Printed and bound in the United States

CONTENTS

ACKNOWLEDGMENTS

A religion, on its doctrinal side, can thus be defined as a system of general truths which have the effect of transforming character when they are sincerely held and vividly apprehended. In the long run your character and your conduct of life depend upon your intimate convictions.[1]

Despite the challenging theological language of Alfred North Whitehead and some of his followers, process theology can be accessible to students, laypeople, and pastors as well as academics; but, more importantly, process theology can be life-transforming. I am a process theologian, who has integrated writing, teaching, preaching, administration, pastoral care, and spiritual direction, for over thirty years. I teach process theology at the seminary and graduate school level. But, I also preach process theology to literate urban congregations and unlettered rural churches. I have come to believe that good theology presents a life-changing vision that can be expressed in the language of laypersons as well as scholars. Anyone who reflects on the interplay of life, death, and suffering, or ponders the meaning of her or his life or personal vocation is, by definition, a theologian. Process theology provides an insightful and inspirational way to express the deepest truths of Christianity as these truths relate to the nature of God; the relationship between divine and human power; the transforming influence of Jesus Christ in a pluralistic, post-modern age; the scope and nature of salvation; the interplay of faith and science; the vocation of the church; and the challenges of ethical decision making. Process theology presents a transformative vision of reality that is responsive to the challenges of postmodernity, pluralism, and technology.

My approach to process theology reflects my experience as a pastor-theologian, committed to spiritual formation, social justice, confessional pluralism, and the healing ministry of Jesus. In addition to my academic appointment, until recently I served as co-pastor of an emerging Christian congregation, committed to welcoming and affirming all of God's children, regardless of ethnicity, gender, theological viewpoint, or sexual identity. The lens through which I view process theology involves openness to healing and wholeness, religious diversity, social justice, and mystical experience. While I describe myself as a progressive Christian, my faith has been shaped by my evangelical roots, mystical experiences, the Christian spiritual tradition, post-modern theology and spirituality, Buddhist and Hindu spiritual practices, and complementary and global medicine. These experiences shape my interpretation of process theology and its importance for twenty-first century Christian faith. Process theology has shaped my character and conduct of life as a pastor, professor, husband, father, and citizen.

Process theology can be perplexing, but it can also be explained in ways that illuminate the experience of laypersons and pastors as well as academics. Freed from its unique and virtually incomprehensible language, process theology presents a vision of a God-filled universe which affirms mystical experiences and surprising, naturalistic expressions of divine power. More than that, process theology presents an open-ended vision of the universe and human life in contrast to many traditional academic and popular theologies, which assert that God determines in eternity every event in our lives. Process theology asserts that God does not and cannot control everything. Rather, than being bad news, process theologians believe that the reality of divine limitation opens the door to greater human creativity and responsibility. We have a role as God's companions in healing the planet. With its emphasis on God's creative-responsive love and relationship to all creation, process theology provides a bridge joining progressive and evangelical Christians in a common ethical and spiritual cause.

This book is the product of nearly forty years of studying process theology. I first encountered process theology in 1971 at San Jose State University in California. As a sophomore, I had the opportunity of taking a course in process theology from Professor Richard Keady in the Religion Department. Later that academic year, I participated in a seminar on the Philosophy of Charles Hartshorne, taught by

CHAPTER 1

WHAT IS PROCESS THEOLOGY AND WHY IS IT SO PERPLEXING?

Religion is the art and theory of the internal life of man, so far as it depends on the man himself and on what is permanent in the nature of things.[1]

Does Theology Matter? Each Sunday, Pastor Lon Solomon of McLean Bible Church in Northern Virginia, pauses for a moment after finishing his exegetical commentary and theological reflection to cue his congregation to respond in one voice with the words, "So what?" This congregational call and response technique is an apt challenge for any theologian or theological movement that seeks to inspire meaning for persons in the twenty first century.

Postmodernism cautions us that all theology is concrete, situational, and time bound. Postmodern theologians warn us that universal theological statements are abstractions that can be both oppressive and irrelevant to flesh and blood human beings. There are no large theological or metaphysical visions, according to postmodernism, that apply to all times and places. Accordingly, any viable and healthy theology in the postmodern era recognizes that it has a perspective that both reflects and shapes our values and behavior. All theological reflection, for good or ill, joins vision and practice in ways that condition how we think and live, individually and corporately. Every theologian's work, accordingly, begs the question, "So what?"

Process theologians affirm that people can still tell a universal story, but, along with postmodernism, they also recognize that this story is grounded in experience and perspective, and must be open-ended and liberating, if it is to be of value for twenty-first century persons. In this introductory chapter, I will set the stage for this text's focus on process theology as resource for creative theological reflection, spiritual practice, and ethical decision-making, by discussing: (1) the importance of theological reflection, (2) the origins of process theology in the work of Alfred North Whitehead, (3) major figures in process theology, and (4) basic principles of process theology. My goal will be to make process theology come alive in ways that are both accessible and relevant to laypersons and pastors as well as academics. In the spirit of postmodernism, my approach will be to describe the many voices of process theology in dialogue with my own vision of process theology as a resource for healing, spiritual formation, social change, and individual and congregational transformation.

THE IMPORTANCE OF THEOLOGICAL REFLECTION

Whether or not we are aware of it, all of us think theologically whenever we try to discern the meaning of our lives, fathom the reality of suffering and tragedy, and discover our place in the universe. Despite the universality of theological reflection, the technical language and conceptuality employed by most theologians is often perplexing to educated laypersons and pastors, who are tempted to ask what difference theology makes for the living of our days. Process theology is often described as incomprehensible to laypersons, in spite of its claim to arise from reflection on human experience—everyday, scientific, and religious. George Bernard Shaw is reputed to have stated that the professions are conspiracies against the laity, and this complaint can easily be leveled at those who employ the intricate and often obscure language of process theology. Laypersons often shake their heads in bewilderment when they hear process theologians try to explain their theological insights with words such as "concrescence," "prehension," "primordial, consequent, and superjective natures of God," "initial aim," and "hybrid physical feelings." While process thought's esoteric language is intended to reflect the novel world view articulated by process theology, many readers barely get through the first paragraphs of works by Alfred North Whitehead, Charles Hartshorne, and their philosophical and theological followers before giving up in frustration. The highly technical language of process theology has led North America's leading process theologian, John Cobb, professor emeritus at the Claremont School of

Theology and Graduate University, to write a Whiteheadian diction- ary to make process theology comprehensible to layperson and pro- fessional alike.[2]

Still, I am convinced that process theology can be accessible to introductory students, laypersons, and pastors. Any theology which claims to describe the ultimate generalities that characterize our lives must ultimately mirror people's language and ordinary experience. In over thirty years of professional life, in which I have integrated class- room and pulpit, computer and hospital bedside, and contemplation and action, as a seminary and college professor, administrator, pas- tor, and process theologian, I have learned that theology, at its best, seeks to transform people's lives by providing an insightful vision of reality that enables persons to find meaning, inspiration, and challenge. I have found this connection between theological vision and spiritual and ethical practices especially to be true for the move- ment in contemporary theology described as process theology. Once persons begin to understand process theology's innovative ways of describing God's relationship with the world, the problem of evil, human creativity, and freedom, and the ethical and spiritual signific- ance of non-human world, they recognize the unique contribution that process theology makes to understand religious life, social trans- formation, and ethical behavior. They also discover how different process theology is from more traditional theologies, including the theologies that may have shaped their lives as children and young adults.

As a working pastor-professor for over thirty years, I have found that theology matters most when it addresses matters of life and death, both physical and spiritual. When people try to make theo- logical and personal sense life's inevitable challenges to our spiritual, emotional, physical, and relational well-being, then theology comes alive and can change peoples' lives. An accessible and insightful theology responds to the perplexities that threaten to overwhelm us intellectually, emotionally, relationally, and spiritually as we face what Episcopal priest Alan Jones has referred to as the "unfixable" events of life.[3] The following encounters reveal why theology is important and why the new ways of looking at God, the world, and ourselves suggested by process theology can transform peoples' lives and inspire hope and creativity in difficult situations.

Helen knocked on my seminary study door one snowy winter afternoon. She immediately confessed that she had trouble believing in the God of her childhood, whose character had been unquestioned throughout most of her life. When Helen's nine year old daughter was diagnosed with a rare form of cancer, she sought the counsel of her Baptist pastor, who challenged her to "Have faith in God," and then added, "Remember, Jesus' words to the woman with the flow of blood, 'your faith has made you well.' If you just trust God, your daughter will get well." When her daughter's condition continued to deteriorate, he suggested that her lack of faith and questions about God's purpose for the illness might be the reason for her daughter's tenuous health condition. He also counseled her that "God has a plan for everything that happens and that her daughter's illness was intended to test of her family's faith. If they passed the test, they would all be spiritually stronger, and her daughter would recover." Beneath the surface was an implied threat: if they failed to have sufficient, unquestioning faith, her daughter would die.

As her daughter's condition continued to show no improvement, the theological counsel Helen received from her pastor and the theological world view of her childhood no longer worked for her. Trying to make theological sense of her daughter's condition, Helen realized that according to her pastor's viewpoint, "Either I'm to blame for her illness, or God has chosen to test us beyond our abilities." And, then, she became angry, "Why would a loving God intentionally hurt my daughter to test my faith? It's not fair! I would never do this to my daughter and I don't believe that a loving God would ever hurt a child to test her parents." Helen's search for a cure took her to a new age healer, who promised that if Helene focused on positive spiritual affirmations, she would find peace and her daughter will get well; but then, like the Baptist pastor, berated her for her "negative thinking" when her daughter's condition remained tenuous. As if to take Helen off the hook for her spiritual immaturity, the healer added one more explanation for her daughter's condition: "Perhaps her illness is the result of something that happened in a previous lifetime. Your daughter is sick because you and your daughter made a prenatal spiritual agreement to deal with issues of suffering in this lifetime. Your daughter chose to be sick so that both of you could learn certain spiritual lessons."

With a countenance mirroring the wintry gloom of the day, Helen came to me, as a last resort, with the question, "Am I really fully responsible for my daughter's health? If so, I'm not spiritually strong enough to change her health condition. If this is a matter of my spiritual maturity, what can I do to help her get well?" Over the course of several meetings, she reflected on her childhood images of God as a distant judge and task master, ready to condemn her for the slightest doubt or misdeed. She also confessed her fear that she might be condemned to hell because of her questions about God's nature and apparently inscrutable purposes for her daughter's illness.

Helen came to realize that the Baptist pastor and new age healer, despite what seemed like profound theological differences, both believed that her daughter's illness was directly the result of our sinfulness or negativity and that somehow God's plan or the inexorable working out of karma was at the root of her child's suffering. Together, we explored the possibility of alternative images of God and explanations of suffering which avoided the pitfalls of explaining her daughter's illness as the result of divine punishment or negative thinking. We also considered the possibility that God neither caused nor wanted her daughter to suffer, but that God is the source of healing possibilities and compassionate companionship. We explored the possibility that God might not be in control of everything that happens in life, and that chance, reflected in the impact of DNA and environmental factors, as well as human and divine purpose shapes our lives. While Helen is still seeking to find a God she can trust to be her and her daughter's companion as they face the medical treatments that lie ahead, she has come to realize that "the only God I can trust is a God who loves us rather than constantly tests us, and accepts our imperfections and tries to help us do better." Our conversations about the alternative vision of God found in process theology have given her hope that she can find a God who is truly on her and her daughter's side, a God who unambiguously wants her daughter to get well.

In pondering the challenges that confront persons like Helen, many popular spiritual leaders proclaim without apology that everything—from good health to personal trauma—comes from the hand of God. As Rick Warren, author of the best-selling *Purpose Driven Life*, asserts, "God has planned every detail of your life *without your input.*"[4] According to Warren, all the most important events of our lives, even the most painful ones, are "father-filtered" and intended for our growth.[5] God not only allows us to experience pain, but places challenging and painful experiences in our lives as opportunities for spiritual growth and tests of our fidelity to God. God smiles on us when we obey "him" and follow without deviation the script that "he" has written in advance.[6] Even though God is the ultimate source of the tragedies that we face, failure to find our purpose in life and deviating from God's clearly discernable plan for our lives leads to meaninglessness in this life and divine punishment in the afterlife.[7] While images of a God who plans everything in our lives may be comforting to some persons, others come to hate a God who determines everything and punishes those who respond inadequately to God's tests of their faith.

Other Christians try to explain God's purposes for history and planet earth in terms of an inexorable divine plan, encompassing past, present, and future. When we met at a local Lancaster, Pennsylvania, coffee house, Steve noted that a recent experience had literally scared the hell out of him. He had heard that I was interested in eschatology, the study of the "last things" or the "end of the world," and what humans might hope for at the end of their lives or the end of planetary history. Steve wondered what I thought about best sellers such as Tim LaHaye's *Left Behind* series, which claims that God will rescue the faithful prior to a time of planetary cataclysm.[8] After a few minutes of general conversation with Steve, I realized that his interest was personal as well as intellectual. Recently, one of his friends had warned him that unless he accepted Jesus as his personal savior; recited a sinner's prayer in which he admitted his unworthiness and powerlessness to change his life; confessed his faith in Jesus; and believed the Bible in its entirety, he would be "left behind" along with the rest of the unbelievers to face unimaginable pain and punishment when Jesus returned in the next few years. "Is this really true? Is God really going to destroy the earth in the next decade? Will I be punished because of my doubts about Jesus and the Bible?"

Steve and I reflected together over the next few weeks on the nature of God, biblical authority, and the role of humans in shaping the future of our planet. He needed a theology that would give him hope, enable him to face his doubts honestly, and inspire him to be an actor rather than a passive bystander in shaping his own future and the future of the earth. He needed to believe that the words of John 3:16, "for God so loved the world," meant that God would never destroy God's good creation. Steve found that process theology's images of divine-human partnership and creativity enabled him to see the future as challenging, but open, and shaped, to some degree, by our personal and corporate actions, rather than being fated for destruction by an arbitrary divine decision.

Many Christians struggle to reconcile their understanding of Christian faith with current scientific discoveries. Audrey was a refugee from a fundamentalist denomination. Now, in thirties, she had become a much respected scientist. Recently, she had begun to ponder cosmology and the origins of the universe. While she could not accept her childhood faith's belief in a "young earth," no more than 10,000 years old, and its identification of evolution with atheism, she was equally dissatisfied with atheistic denials of purpose in the universe, suggested by many in the scientific community. As a scientist, she had come to recognize that the "elegant universe"[9] she studied at both the microcosmic and macrocosmic levels could not solely be the result of a purposeless cosmic accident. She admitted to me that she believed that "there's some sort of wisdom at work in the evolution of galaxies and our planet." She confessed that she needed to find a world view that honored science and its methodology and yet made room for meaning in the universe. "I know that I can no longer believe in the God I grew up with, but I'm searching for something besides humanity to give meaning to the universe. Can I be a scientist and person of faith, too?" she asked. Audrey chose to audit my class on process theology and explore the possibility that God is the ultimate source of the evolutionary process. She has discovered that faith and science can complement one another and that believing in God can inspire and encourage, rather than censor, human creativity and scientific discovery.

These encounters remind us that theology is not just reserved for scholars, but, as liberation theologians have long told us, emerges from our lived experiences of pain, struggle, and, I would add, personal perplexity. As I said earlier, laypeople enter the world of theological reflection when they ask questions relating to life, death, suffering, and beyond. While we can't help being theologians at such moments, the issue is whether our theologies will lead to hope or despair, and action or passivity, in times of personal and planetary struggle. While I believe that there are a variety of theological resources for hopeful action and meaningful living, this text reflects specifically on the intellectual, spiritual, and ethical resources of process theology for people in the twenty first century.

THE ORIGINS OF PROCESS THEOLOGY: THE VISION OF ALFRED NORTH WHITEHEAD

Process theology describes the dynamic interplay of permanence and flux, evident in the universe and our own lives. As we will see later in this chapter, following World War I, theology became important to Alfred North Whitehead, the intellectual parent of process philosophy and theology, who expanded his philosophical focus from mathematics and science to metaphysics and religion to make sense of his son's death. In pondering the dynamic nature of life, Whitehead asserts:

> That "all things flow" is the first vague generalization which the unsystematized, barely analyzed, intuition of men has produced. It is the theme of some of the best Hebrew poetry in the Psalms; it appears as one of the first generalizations of Greek philosophy in the form of the saying of Heraclitus; amid the later barbarism of Anglo Saxon thought it reappears in the story of the sparrow flitting through the banqueting hall of the Northumbrian king; and in all stages of civilization its recognition lends its pathos to poetry . . . the flux of things is one ultimate generalization around which we must weave our philosophical system.[10]

But, within the flow of life, there is a complementary notion; just as novelty requires order to give meaning and stability to life, flux requires something permanent to provide a sense of confidence that our actions truly matter in the scheme of things.

> The other notion dwells on permanences of things—the solid earth, the mountains, the stones, the Egyptian pyramids, the spirit of man, God. The best rendering of integral experience, expressing its general form divested of irrelevant details, is often to be found in the utterances of religious aspiration.[11]

Whitehead cites the first two lines of a famous hymn as expressing the reality that "in the inescapable flux, there is something that abides; in the overwhelming permanence, there is an element that escapes into flux."[12]

> Abide with me,
> Fast falls the eventide.[13]

Whitehead's philosophy reflects his experience of permanence and flux, revealed in the eclipse of Newtonian physics, the decline British Empire, and the emergence of quantum physics. Born in 1861, the son of an Anglican clergyman and schoolmaster, Alfred North Whitehead, no doubt reflected on the interplay of eternity and temporality in conversations with his father. As an adult, he gained notoriety initially as a mathematician and philosopher of science. He garnered international recognition as the co-author and mathematical partner with philosopher Bertrand Russell of the multi-volume *Principia Mathematica,* their attempt to provide the theoretical foundations for mathematics and symbolic logic. Whitehead taught at the universities of Cambridge and London, before accepting an invitation to teach philosophy at Harvard University (1924–1937).

Though he spent many years as a religious agnostic, Whitehead considered joining the Roman Catholic Church in his mid-thirties. But, as Victor Lowe, Whitehead's primary biographer, notes, the crumbling of Newtonian physics turned Whitehead's scientific and religious worlds upside down. Henceforth, Whitehead would mistrust any attempt at dogmatic certainty whether in science or religion. As Lowe reflects,

> He now could find no clear authority in either Rome or Canterbury, no system of dogmas that satisfied him, and no compelling reasons for subscribing to any promulgated doctrines of Christian faith. He had come to ask himself more and more frequently, "How can they be so sure?" The upshot was that Whitehead became an agnostic.[14]

Even after Whitehead formulated the elegant metaphysical vision that serves as the foundation for process theology's innovative vision of God and the world, he still believed that doctrinal certainty, whether scientific or religious, was the enemy of intellectual growth and adventurous spirituality.

Whitehead remained a philosophical agnostic for nearly a quarter of a century until his personal and intellectual life was shaken by the tragedy of World War I in which the brightest and best young men of his sons' generation were killed on foreign soil. As Lowe asserts, "After World War I, in which many of his pupils and one of his two sons was killed, he gradually developed his own philosophical theism."[15] Like the earlier collapse of Newtonian physics that inspired his agnosticism, the tragedies of war compelled Whitehead to reconsider God, but this time, not in terms of dogmatic certainty, but the tentative vision of God, described in terms of "the supreme monad, not as omnipotent Creator but as eternally *with* it [the world] in two ways . . . the source of all possible values . . . [who] receives, transforms, and keeps forever the monads that have perished in the temporal world; thus God grows with the world, always in process."[16]

In reflecting on Whitehead's religious transformation, Victor Lowe quotes Whitehead's description of religion in *Science and the Modern World*:

Religion is the vision of something which stands beyond, and within, the passing flux of immediate things; something which is real, and yet waiting to be realized; something which is a remote possibility, and yet the greatest of present facts; something that gives meaning to all that passes, and yet eludes apprehension; something whose possession is the final good, and yet is beyond all reach; something which is the ultimate ideal, and the hopeless quest.[17]

In his commentary on this passage, Lowe asserts that "[t]he author was *looking for something,* something that will give meaning to what has happened; in Whitehead's case, to the carnage of the First World War, and Eric's death in it."[18] Whitehead's spiritual journey led him to Harvard where he planted the philosophical seeds that grew into the theological movement, known as process theology, through texts such as *Science and the Modern World, Religion in the Making, Process and Reality, Adventures in Ideas, Function of Reason,* and *Modes of Thought*.

Some of the perplexity readers find in process theology, involves the adoption by later process theologians, of Whitehead's unique philosophical language. Whitehead believed that his break with his philosophical predecessors, especially in their understanding of the mind-body relationship, the nature and scope of experience, sense perception, and the relationship of God with the world, required new and unfamiliar ways of expression. As theologian John Cobb notes:

No deeply original thinking can be expressed adequately in existing language. That language operates among people who see the world in a particular way. The deeply original thought leads to a different way of seeing the world. It has to work against the implications of the existing language. It has to draw the readers or hearers into noticing features of experience that have heretofore eluded them. It has to evoke to consciousness dim intuitions that have been suppressed by the existing conceptuality and socialization. One cannot translate the new vision into the vocabulary of the old. In Jesus' words, this would be to pour new wine into old wineskins.[19]

The challenge of reading Whitehead and following the language of process philosophy and theology is embodied in a humorous recollection of Whitehead's 1928 Gifford Lectures, which were later published as *Process and Reality*, the foundational text of process theology. Dr. J.M. Whittaker wrote the following to Victor Lowe:

[Eddington] was a marvelous popular lecturer who had enthralled an audience of 600 for his entire course. The same audience turned up to Whitehead's first lecture but it was completely unintelligible, not only to the world at large but to the elect. My father remarked to me afterwards that if he had not known Whitehead well he would have suspected that it was an imposter making it up as he went along (this had actually happened in a lecture in Psychology at Oxford shortly before). The audience at subsequent lectures was only about half a dozen at all, so I am told, for I fear that I myself was one of the backsliders.[20]

While some persons judge theology primarily in terms of the question "can it preach?" the philosophical foundations of much of modern theology present challenges to theologians as well as clergy and laypersons, beginning first with the questions, "can it be understood?" and, then, "can it be shared with others?" I have been rewarded as a constructive theologian by hours spent with texts such as Whitehead's *Process and Reality,* Immanuel Kant's *Critique of Pure Reason,* G.W.F. Hegel's *Phenomenology of Spirit*, and Martin Heidegger's *Being and Time* as well as texts in quantum physics and Christian mysticism, all of which are intellectual challenges to lay and academic readers alike. Although I will seek in this introductory text to provide an accessible guide for the perplexed and an interpretation of process theology in the context of our dynamic postmodern world, I must admit, nevertheless, that even the most accessible introduction requires the creative transformation of Whitehead's language in ways that will both challenge and inspire the reader. Without compromising the spirit of Whitehead's metaphysics and process theology, I hope to present process theology using Whitehead's technical language only when necessary and, then, always accompanied by an accessible and experience-based definition.

Shortly before his death on December 30, 1947, Whitehead, in conversation with his first biographer Lucien Price, shared poetic words that embody the spirit of process theology. It is the spirit of Whitehead's intimate and relational God that I hope to evoke throughout this text.

> God is *in* the world, or nowhere, creating continually in us and around us. The creative principle is everywhere, in animate and so-called inanimate matter, in the ether, water, earth, human hearts. But this creation is a creative process, and "the process is itself the actuality," since no sooner than you arrive you start on a fresh journey. Insofar as man partakes of this creative process does he partake of the divine, of God, and that participation is his immortality, reducing the question of whether his individuality survives the death of his body to the estate of an irrelevancy. His true destiny as a cocreator of the universe is his dignity and his grandeur.[21]

FIVE LEADERS IN THE FORMATION OF PROCESS THEOLOGY: HARTSHORNE, COBB, PITTENGER, LOOMER, AND GRIFFIN[22]

Alfred North Whitehead planted the seeds of a theological movement that continues to transform mainstream, progressive, and open and relational evangelical Christianity. Whitehead's vision initially inspired a group of philosophers and theologians who sought to embody his metaphysical ideas in the formation of new visions of God, the world, the relationship of religion and science, human existence, interfaith dialogue, sexuality, and congregational life. The five figures I've cited as key figures in the development of process theology, span three generations of process theology from the philosophical theology of Charles Hartshorne to the constructive postmodernism of David Griffin. I will briefly describe the unique contribution of each of these persons to the emergence of process theology and their important contribution to the unfolding of process theology. I had the honor of studying with John Cobb, Bernard Loomer, and David

Ray Griffin at Claremont Graduate University and School of Theology, where I also heard lectures and participated in informal conversations with Norman Pittenger and Charles Hartshorne. While I could have chosen other theologians such as Schubert Ogden, Bernard Meland, Daniel Day Williams, and Henry Nelson Wieman as representative of process theology, I believe that these five figures have had the greatest impact on the formation and spread of process theology throughout the world.

Charles Hartshorne (1897–2000). Also the child of an Episcopalian/Anglican priest, Charles Hartshorne's philosophical adventure can be broadly described as an extended meditation on the relationship of God and the world.[23] Hartshorne adopted Anselm's ontological argument which asserted that if we can conceive of a being, such as God, who is greater than anything that can exist or the mind can conceive, then that being must of necessity exist. In contrast to those who understand God's perfection as unchanging and entirely complete, thus, either requiring no input from the world or having determined everything that will exist prior to creation, Hartshorne affirmed that God is unsurpassable except in terms of God's future states. Accordingly, God is constantly growing in God's experience and response to the evolving universe. Following Whitehead, Hartshorne asserted that God is, by definition, the most relative of beings: God shapes all things by God's influence on every moment of experience and God is influenced by all things as the one to whom all hearts are open and all desires known.

Hartshorne is noted for his identification of *panentheism*, or "all things in God," as the most faithful and philosophical word to describe God's ongoing relationship with the world. Accordingly, Hartshorne contrasts panentheism with three other ways to understand God's relationship to the world:

1. *Deism*—the belief that God creates the world, like a watchmaker, and then withdraws to let the world take its course, observing but never acting in a world whose ongoing history is determined entirely by creaturely activity.
2. *Theism*—the belief in an unchanging God, external to the world, who nevertheless miraculously and supernaturally acts in the world at specific moments in its history.
3. *Pantheism*—the belief that God and the world constitute one reality, essentially indistinguishable from one another.

Hartshorne describes God as the soul of the world, dynamically moving through God's cosmic body, giving it life and direction, while constantly receiving and responding to the body's condition. God embraces the world in its entirety, but is always more than the evolving world. In this dynamic process of divine call and creaturely response, we can affirm "God in all things" as the source of inspiration and possibility and "all things in God" in terms of God's preservation of all things in the divine memory.

In his reflections on the nature of God, Hartshorne also distinguished between the absolute and relative aspects of God's unfolding relationship with the world. God's character, described in terms of universal love, omnipresence, and omniscience is unchanging and eternal, while God's experience and response to the world is constantly changing. Hartshorne believes that the insights of process theology and philosophy truly embody the biblical affirmation that "God is love." Hartshorne's metaphysics of love reflects the vision of a sympathetic God who embraces our lives in their fullness and responds by shaping the divine vision and experience to the relativities of our world.

Norman Pittenger (1905–1997). Whereas Whitehead moved from England to the United States after a long academic career, Norman Pittenger retired to England after a distinguished academic career at General Theological Seminary in New York. From 1966 until his death, Pittenger was an Honorary Senior Member of Kings College, Cambridge. An Episcopalian/Anglican priest, Pittenger saw his mission as introducing process theology to the church and exploring the resources of process theology for understanding major Christian themes such as the nature of God, Christology, the Holy Spirit, the Trinity, prayer, sin, worship, sexuality, and human nature. In the spirit of process theology's affirmation of God's universal quest for beauty and wholeness, Pittenger was one of the first theologians to affirm that homosexuality and homosexual relationships were consistent with Christian faith. God's aim at beauty, intimately connected with complexity and vibrancy of experience, embraces diversity in sexuality, intimacy, and creativity in the human and non-human world.

Bernard Loomer (1912–1985). One of the highpoints of my graduate studies at Claremont Graduate University was my participation in the "Advanced Seminar on Process Theology," taught by Bernard Loomer in Spring of 1978. Each week as he drew on his pipe, Loomer regaled our class, which included some of the makers of contemporary process theology, Rita Nakashima Brock, Bruce Epperly, Catherine Keller, and Rebecca Ann Parker, with his expansive vision of process theology.[24] We were not alone in being inspired by Loomer. Although he never published a full-length book, Loomer's impact on the development of process theology came through his influence on his students at the University of Chicago, Pacific School of Religion and Graduate Theological Union, and the Claremont Graduate University and Claremont School of Theology. In fact, Loomer was credited by Charles Hartshorne as the source of the term "process theology," although Loomer noted later that "process-relational theology" more aptly described his understanding of the theological movement he helped shape.

Empirical in orientation, Loomer took a different path than the more rationalistic perspectives of Hartshorne, Cobb, and Griffin. For Loomer size, relationship, and experience were central themes. Theology, ethics, and personal growth should alike be judged in terms of their stature, that is, their ability to embrace as much of reality in its diversity as possible without losing one's identity or spiritual center. Stature, as a theological concept, shapes our understanding of relationships and power dynamics. According to Loomer, divine and human power dynamics can be described either as relational or coercive. Relational understandings of power are receptive as well as creative and embrace the reality of otherness, while coercive understandings of power are unilateral and seek to minimize or eliminate the impact of others on the one who wields power. In speaking of God's nature, Loomer comes close to affirming a form of pantheism in which God is the living energy embracing all things. Rather than being fully and unambiguously good, as most process theologians assert, Loomer's God is the ambiguous energy of creation, seeking the fullness of life, yet embracing both the creative and destructive aspects of the universe. According to Loomer, a fully concrete God of sufficient stature must be identified with the whole of life and not just the positive and life-supportive aspects of creation.

John Cobb (1925–).[25] The child of Methodist missionaries in Japan, Cobb experienced a crisis of faith at the University of Chicago, which led him to pursue graduate studies at the Divinity School where he found a "no-holds-barred inquiry centered around the common concern for fresh, contemporary articulation of the Christian faith."[26] Cobb notes that "through Hartshorne, I encountered the still richer and more complex conceptuality of Alfred North Whitehead, and I have been living with him ever since."[27]

Cobb's ministerial and missionary background enabled him to explore both the theoretical and practical aspects of process theology. Cobb's *A Christian Natural Theology* and *Christ in a Pluralistic Age* are considered classics in process theology. Over five decades, Cobb's theology embodies what Loomer described as "size" insofar as Cobb drew connections between process theology and ecology, economics, anthropology, theological education, spirituality, and interfaith dialogue. Cobb's work joins intellectual precision with openness to piety and mysticism. Perhaps more than any theologian in the last fifty years, Cobb has personally and theologically integrated Buddhism and Christianity as a model for sound and mutually enriching interfaith dialogue. At the heart of Cobb's work is the vision of Christ as the principle of creative transformation which inspires the world toward greater beauty, inclusiveness, and justice. Creative transformation, embodied in the historical Jesus as well as throughout the universe, embraces both the richness of the past and gifts of tradition, whether in a religion, congregation, family, or personal life, in light of God's ongoing quest for wholeness and stature in the microcosm and macrocosm. On a personal note, Cobb has been for me the model of lived theology; his care for his students and respect for colleagues and laypeople reflects the relational aspect of process theology at its best.

David Ray Griffin (1939–).[28] David Griffin has become one of the leading voices in constructive postmodern theology. Similar to my own story, Griffin found process theology essential in his quest to find a faith worth believing and an alternative to the conservative theology of his childhood. Also, similar to my own experiences a decade later, process theology inspired Griffin to join East and West and mysticism and ethics. Griffin's text *God, Power, and Evil* remains the most influential interpretation of the problem of evil from the perspective of process theology. Recognizing that neither deconstructive postmodernism nor reductionist modernism, both of which make God-talk a virtual impossibility, can creatively respond to the intellectual and planetary crises of the contemporary world, Griffin articulates what he describes as a constructive postmodernism, which embraces the insights of ancient, medieval, modern, and postmodern thought from the perspective of a Whiteheadian vision of reality. According to Griffin, Whitehead's vision provides a constructive, yet humble, metaphysical vision through its emphasis on the following: the interdependence of life, non-sensory experience as the primary mode of perception (the experience of causal relationships, or unconscious causal efficacy, as prior to and foundational for the more sophisticated experiences of presentational immediacy), non-local causation (action at a distance, thus, making room for mystical experiences and the impact of intercessory prayer on other persons), panexperientialism (the affirmation that all concrete actualities embody some level of experience), the continuity of mind and body, theistic naturalism, and panentheism (the affirmation that God is immanent within the creative process, working within the dynamic, evolving, and contextual laws of nature). Like Pittenger and Cobb, Griffin has explored the resources of process theology for Christology, the problem of evil, science, mysticism and paranormal experiences, politics, and globalism.

THE ONGOING ADVENTURES OF PROCESS THEOLOGY

The adventure of process theology continues in the work of the Center for Process Studies in Claremont, California. Founded in 1973 by John Cobb and David Griffin to explore "the relevance of process thought to many fields of action and reflection," the Center for Process Studies seeks to "promote the common good by means of the relational approach found in process thought," inspired by Alfred North Whitehead and Charles Hartshorne.[29] Process and Faith, a program of the Center for Process Studies, is "dedicated to providing practical applications of process-relational theology to all aspects of faith life: spirituality, education, preaching and worship, biblical interpretation, counseling, and ministries of justice."[30] As the primary vehicle for sharing the resources of process theology to religious communities, Process and Faith grounds its work in the affirmation of God's creative presence in all things, including the world's great religious traditions:

We believe the world is relational and interdependent, that God is present in every moment of experience, and that our choices really do make a difference. We are Protestants, Catholics, Unitarians, Jews, Buddhists, and Muslims who have discovered that process-relational theology—which is a way of understanding God and the world—makes sense. It encourages us to deepen our particular faith while reaching out with respect to other faiths for inter-religious dialogue and shared ministries.

The evolution of process theology continues not only in North America, but in China and Europe. Over the last two decades, impact of process theology has expanded through the creative and insightful work of theologians such as Clark Williamson, Marjorie Suchocki, Jay McDaniel, Philip Clayton, Bruce Epperly, Rita Nakashima Brock, Catherine Keller, and Monica Coleman; biblical scholars such as Ron Farmer, David Lull, and Will Beardslee; philosopher-theologians such as Lewis Ford and Robert Mesle as well as scores of younger scholars, pastors, and persons who are shaping the next adventures of process theology.

KEY THEMES IN PROCESS THEOLOGY

Marjorie Suchocki, dean and professor of theology emeritus at Claremont School of Theology, noted that "it is not a question of *whether* theology will be used, but *which* philosophy will be used."[31] Truly there is no such thing as a purely biblical or experiential theo-logy. As John Wesley and his followers asserted, we understand God's presence in our lives and the world through our reflections on and experience of the dynamic interplay of scripture, reason, experience, and tradition, to which I would also add culture, our ongoing achieve-ments in literature, science, medicine, and other religious traditions. For two millennia, Christian theologians have employed philosophy as a way of making sense of God's revelation in scripture, the adventures of the Hebraic people, the life of Jesus, and the experi-ences of first followers of Jesus. Whereas in the past, Christian theologians found inspiration in the insights of Plato, Aristotle, and Neo-Platonism, contemporary theologians have formulated their understanding of Christianity in terms of the insights of philoso-phers such as Immanuel Kant, G.W.F. Hegel, and Martin Heidegger. Each of these philosophers has shaped the unfolding of Christian theology in particular ways. Process theology is no exception to the impact of philosophy in understanding, interpreting, and transform-ing Christian theology for our current context. Process theologians believe that the philosophical insights of Alfred North Whitehead and Charles Hartshorne provide the most adequate way of interpret-ing Christian faith in our pluralistic, postmodern, scientifically, and technologically adventurous world. In the following paragraphs, I will describe the basic principles of process theology as a prelude to reflecting in the remainder of this text on more specific aspects of Christian faith. In particular, I will focus on the following: (1) the nature of philosophical and theological thinking, (2) the primacy of process, (3) dynamic interdependence, (4) the universality of experience, (5) creativity and freedom, and (6) God as the primary exemplification of the metaphysical principles pertaining to all things.

The Nature of Philosophical Thinking. Whereas postmodernism questions any all-encompassing metaphysical description, Whitehead invited philosophers to think big, yet recognize the relativity and limitations of their discipline. In the spirit of the apostle Paul's affirmation that we have this treasure in earthen vessels (2 Corinthians 4:7), Whitehead believed that we can frame a vision of reality that makes sense of our world, but is always subject to correction and change. According to Whitehead, "speculative philosophy [or metaphysics] is an endeavor to frame a coherent, logical, necessary system of general ideas in terms of which every element of our experience can be interpreted."[32] The philosophical crucible within which theology finds its interpretation must, accordingly, be profoundly concrete and experiential in nature. Whitehead states that the "true method of discovery is like the flight of an airplane. It starts from the ground of particular observation; it makes a flight into the thin air of imaginative generalization; and it again lands for renewed observation, rendered acute by rational interpretation."[33] Yet, the lover of wisdom, in spirit of the philosopher Socrates, is constantly aware of her or his ignorance: "Metaphysical categories are not dogmatic statements of the obvious; they are tentative formulations of ultimate generalities."[34] In contrast to the "static dogmatism" that Whitehead identifies with certain types of mathematics and religion, "[r]ationalism is an adventure in the clarification of thought, progressive, and never final. But it is an adventure in which even partial success has importance."[35] Accordingly, Whitehead's metaphysics and process theology exhibit what Robert Mesle describes as "bold humility."[36]

In Christian theology and mysticism, this interplay of theological insight and humility is reflected in the dynamic interplay of the *apophatic,* "without images," and *kataphatic*, "with images," approach to understanding God. Long before the postmodern critique of attempts to articulate a universal metaphysic, Christian theologians recognized that our religious experiences reveal something important about God's nature, even though no image or word about God is ever final. The grandeur and diversity of the universe that inspire the philosophical and theological adventure remind us "how shallow, puny, and imperfect are efforts to sound the depths of the nature of things. In philosophical discussion, the merest hint of dogmatic certainty as to the finality of statement is an exhibition of folly."[37]

Like Carl Jung in the field of psychology, Whitehead challenged the identification of religion with pathology and immaturity. Religious experience and practice provide important data for metaphysical reflection. According to Whitehead:

> Philosophy frees itself from the taint of ineffectiveness by its close relations with religion and with science, natural and sociological. It attains its chief importance by fusing the two, namely, religion and science, into one rational scheme of thought . . . . Religion is the translation of general ideas into particular thoughts, particular emotions, and particular purposes; it is directed to the end of stretching individual interest beyond its self-defeating particularity. Philosophy finds religion and modifies it; and conversely religion is among the data of experience which philosophy must weave into its own scheme.[38]

Whitehead goes so far as to say that the mystical experiences and moments of transcendence from which religious traditions emerge, rare as they are, are not aberrations but provide insight into the nature of reality.[39] I believe that if Whitehead were alive today he would include studies of paranormal experiences, near death experiences, and the relationship of spirituality and neuroscience along with the insights of legitimate spiritual healers and complementary medical practitioners as data for both theological and philosophical reflection. Philosophy must join imagination and concreteness in the framing of an adequate vision of reality, subject always to revision, transformation, and expansion, and embracing with postmodernism the many narratives and experiences of the world, in its unfolding adventures of ideas.

Reality as Dynamic Process. Process philosophy and theology describes our world in terms of ongoing creative transformation in every moment of experience ranging from your current experience of reading this text to God's ongoing and all-encompassing experience of the evolving universe as it embraces both your experience of reading this text and the experiences of all other creatures. Whereas some philosophers identify metaphysical perfection and ultimate reality with eternal changelessness or affirm the existence of an unchanging self beneath the accidents of daily experience, process theologians and philosophers believe that the constantly changing and evolving world of experience, joining unity and diversity in each momentary event, constitutes reality in its concreteness. Spiritual life is not a flight from the realm of change and diversity, but the discovery and joyful embrace of beauty, creativity, and eternity within the temporal world. The soul is not an unchanging substance that observes its experiences from a spiritual distance. Rather, process theology describes the soul as a stream of experiences, always creative and always connected with God's ongoing and intimate vision for each drop in the stream. Truly the process is the reality, whether it pertains to our personal adventures or God's unfolding movements within the universe.

The world emerges from the dynamic interplay of flux and permanence, in which the eternal and unchanging finds its relevance through its relationship to the temporal and changing world, and the temporal and changing finds completion in its role as contributing to the ongoing universe, embraced by God's everlasting and ever-expanding experience of the universe. As we will see, God is not the exception to the dynamic nature of the universe, but rather the dynamic God-world relationship is the primary example of creaturely experience in its many expressions.

Process involves the emergence of novelty. Temporality brings new experiences to God and to the creaturely world. Accordingly, the future is not predetermined but open and surprising for us and also for God. A living God experiences new things and does new things. Present as the inspiration of every emerging moment of experience, God is the source of novelty, whose loving mercies are "new every morning" (Lamentations 3:23) in God's ongoing relationship with the world. In our dynamic and ever-changing world, God is the most dynamic and ever-changing reality; God's becoming embraces the eternal, temporal, and everlasting in an ever-creative, self-surpassing dialogue with the universe.

Dynamic Interdependence. Just as philosophers and theologians have wrestled with the interplay of change and changelessness, they have also pondered what is most definitive of reality and our daily lives, independence or interdependence. The primacy of independence has a long philosophical, ethical, and economic history, enshrined in the notion of a substance, whether God or mortal, as something that requires nothing but itself to exist;[40] the image of the "self-made man" who lifts himself up by his bootstraps and becomes a success without the help of others; and the belief that a person's property, firearms, or body are her or his to dispense with as he or she wishes, without regard to the greater good of the community or planet.

Substance-oriented thinking also has reigned in the world of medicine, in which until recently physicians, following Descartes' affirmation that the mind and body are unrelated, treated the body in isolation from a person's emotions, spiritual life, and environment. While analysis may on occasion require us to look at a particular economic, health, or personal situation in isolation from its environment, process theology and philosophy, like Buddhist metaphysics, asserts that interdependence is the primary reality within whom our lives emerge and to which our lives contribute. You cannot separate the mind or the body, or the person from her or his environment; the health of each is intimately related to the other. The ultimate entities in the universe, Whitehead asserts, are not independent and self-enclosed atoms, but occasions of experience, or actual entities, "drops of experience, complex, and interdependent."[41] In one way or another, the whole universe influences the emergence of each moment of experience.

Reality is profoundly ecological. Process thought asserts that we cannot distinguish where the body ends and the external world begins. The mind shapes the body and embodiment influences mentality. Recognizing the interdependence of life has profound practical consequences. For example, holistic approaches to medicine describe human health as a constantly-changing constellation of interdependent factors, including DNA, emotions, spirituality, relationships with others, economics, environment, all of which must be taken into consideration in promoting the health of people and communities.[42] Our lives emerge from a dynamic of web of relationships in which each moment of experience arises from a creative synthesis or *conscrescence* of its *prehensions,* or experiences of the world, and then contributes to the future of its immediate and ambient world. While solitude is an essential aspect of spiritual experience, metaphysical, ethical, or experiential separation is ultimately an illusion. Still, in contrast to substance-oriented religions and philosophies, often characterized by the extremes of monism, in which only one eternal reality is affirmed, or dualism, in which spirit and matter are ultimately alien from one another, process theology's affirmation of interdependence as a religious and metaphysical principle sees diversity and differentiation, and not uniformity or union, as essential to life. Process theologians believe that the goal of life in an interdependent universe is to experience a widening, and not a dissolving, of self, such that the well-being of others and one's own well-being are intimately connected in the moment by moment and long-term process of self-actualization.

A Universe of Experience. Today we are rediscovering the wonder, beauty, and value of the non-human world on its own terms and apart from human interests. While followers of Newton and Descartes understood the world in accordance with images of clocks and other machines, implicitly denying experience or value to non-human life, process thought begins with experience and organic relatedness. Process theology asserts that whatever ultimately exists, at every level of experience, can be described as an *actual occasion* or *occasion of experience*, each one of which creatively synthesizes or integrates the data from which it emerges.

In many ways, the notion of *panexperientialism*, or the universality of experience, is the most difficult and also one of the most breathtaking and life-transforming aspects of process thought. Process thought advocates a re-enchantment of nature, in which experience, feeling, value, and beauty are understood to be inherent in the nature of things, and not merely the result of our human categories of experience (Immanuel Kant) or relationship with, or use, of non-human realities (Martin Heidegger). Humankind is not the experiential center of the universe nor is humankind alone in a mechanistic and meaningless world, as existentialists suggest; rather, humans are part of a multi-leveled experiential universe, throbbing with emotion and creativity.

When process theologians speak of the universality of experience, they are not claiming that all events are conscious. Consciousness presupposes the universality of experience and is the tip of the iceberg, grounded in unconscious, but nevertheless minimally creative and relational, experiences at every level of life. Rocks and tables, for example, don't experience the world in terms of a central organizing experience or center, such as our minds; but they are nevertheless composed of the dynamic relationships of interdependent occasions of experience, whose apparent stability is ultimately grounded in their essential social relatedness, or resulting from sharing some common character, with one another. Philosopher Robert Mesle describes the nature of experience as it relates to rocks and higher organisms:

> Rocks don't feel pain. Experience is something only individuals have. An electron is probably an individual; a rock is not. Possibly atoms and molecules might be said to be complex individuals. Cells appear to be individuals because they are organized to have a unity of structure and experience that enables them to interact with their environment in purposeful ways. Your mind is an individual. The point here is that rocks and chairs and pens don't have experience any more complex than that of the individual molecules or electrons that compose them.[43] Still, the fact that rocks, tables, computers, and pens are composed of interdependent occasions of experience challenges us to treat them with care and respect.

You only need to look under a microscope to challenge Descartes' notion that the non-human world is unfeeling, disconnected, and inert. Life and experience abound whether in test tubes, in the womb, or in congregants listening to a sermon. Take a few minutes to observe a dog or cat and you will disprove both Descartes' mind-body dualism and his restriction of creative experience to humankind. My two cats, sitting beside the fire this winter morning are not insentient machines, but have purposes and emotions that exist in some continuity with my own. Much of their behavior, like our own, involves stimulus and response, as they eagerly wait for their morning feeding or as I, in similar fashion, look forward to the first cup of predawn coffee, before turning to a morning of study and writing. My cats, nevertheless, initiate new behaviors that surprise my wife Kate and me. Further, as sentient beings, dogs, cats, chickens, and dolphins, experience joy and pain, fear and contentment, and must be given some level of ethical consideration, according to process thought. As process theologian, biblical scholar, and novelist Ron Farmer notes in his novel *Awakening*, pigs raised in factory farms are not merely production units, but experience depression, fear, and pain. Mystical experiences may, as Farmer suggests, open us to the pain and joy that non-humans experience.[44] From this perspective, Jesus' affirmation that God cares for the birds of the air and lilies of the field is justified both metaphysically and ethically. A world in which we can affirm, "let everything that breathes praise God," (Psalm 150:10),[45] invites us to look for experience and value in all things.

Robert Frost gives voice to a vision of panexperientialism, or the universality of experience, in his poem, "A Considerable Speck":

A speck that would have been beneath my sight
On any but a paper sheet so white
Set off across what I had written there.
And I had idly poised my pen in air
To stop it with a period of ink
When something strange about it made me think,
This was no dust speck by my breathing blown,
But unmistakably a living mite
With inclinations it could call its own.
It paused as with suspicion of my pen,
And then came racing wildly on again
To where my manuscript was not yet dry;
Then paused again and either drank or smelt--
With loathing, for again it turned to fly.
Plainly with an intelligence I dealt.
It seemed too tiny to have room for feet,
Yet must have had a set of them complete
To express how much it didn't want to die.
It ran with terror and with cunning crept.
It faltered: I could see it hesitate;
Then in the middle of the open sheet
Cower down in desperation to accept
Whatever I accorded it of fate.
I have none of the tenderer-than-thou
Collectivistic regimenting love
With which the modern world is being swept.
But this poor microscopic item now!
Since it was nothing I knew evil of
I let it lie there till I hope it slept.
I have a mind myself and recognize
Mind when I meet with it in any guise
No one can know how glad I am to find
On any sheet the least display of mind.[46]

Process thought's vision of the universality of experience transforms our understanding of God and our place in the world. On the one hand, there is a continuity of human and non-human experience, reaching back as far as the big bang and the origins of life on earth. All creatures are experientially connected. On the other hand, if all creatures experience the world and their own creative process, minimally speaking, at some deep and primitive emotional level, then God can be perceived as moving *through* all things as a companion and guide, inspiring all creatures toward beauty and fulfillment for themselves and the world from the inside, rather than as an external, dispassionate clockmaker. The continuity and varied complexity of experience, embracing mind and body, and human and non-human, inspires feelings of wonder and humility and opens us to the possibility that just as there are levels of experience less complex and sentient than human experience, there may also be more complex and sensitive levels of experience, interplanetary, angelic, and divine. The universality of experience calls us to be good stewards of a world that has value apart from our use of it. "Reverence for life," as physician and biblical scholar Albert Schweitzer noted, is the appropriate response to a living, experiential universe.

Creativity and Freedom. Experience, relationship, value, creativity, and freedom go hand in hand, according to process thought. To exist is to experience one's environment and thus prefer some things over others as supportive of one's well-being and individual projects. The very process of preference, of noting at some primitive level, what supports or hinders our process of self-creation, points to the universality of creativity and freedom. Process thought avoids extremes in the philosophical debate between absolute freedom and complete determinism. Creativity and freedom are always relational and contextual, never absolute or unfettered. The datum of experience both limits and provides the foundation of our personal creativity.

Whitehead asserts that creativity as the dynamic process of relational self-creation, characterizes all experience, be it divine or creaturely. In each moment, we are artists of our experience, bringing together the many influences of the past into one cohesive whole, which becomes the gift of this unique moment to the universe beyond itself. Guided by interplay of God's intimate vision for each moment of experience and the environment from which it arises, each event is a process of self-creation, or *"concrescence,"* aiming at intensity and beauty of experience for itself and its immediate environment.

As you consider the universality of self-creation, I invite you to reflect on your own experience right now in this "sacrament of the present moment."[47] Consider the complex processes of bodily inheritance, environmental stimuli, and personal intentionality that make up this unique and unrepeatable moment of experience. While other persons, in terms of this momentary experience, may share the same environmental data as we do, none will experience this data with the same feeling tones or unique response as you do. Each one of us weighs the data in different ways, and shapes our experience accordingly. Despite the significant influence of the environment and our past history, we are artists of our own experience, whether or not we are aware of it, shaping our experience in terms of our conscious or unconscious aims and values. The reality of self-creation is an important theological point. In contrast to Rick Warren's theological and spiritual determinism, described in this and the next chapter, process theology asserts that God has *not* planned the most important details of your life in advance without your input, nor does God want you to fulfill a purpose determined in eternity.[48] Rather, God's aim or vision is for you to integrate God's vision of possibility, described in terms of the initial aim, the influence of the environment, and your own evolving creativity moment by moment. While your freedom is radically limited in any given moment of experience by the environmentally-given universe, openness to divine possibility and personal creativity will transform your life over the long haul. Still, despite the significant influence of the past, including our previous decisions, we have the freedom to choose how we respond to the data of our experience. As Victor Frankl notes from the perspective of a Holocaust survivor, "the experiences of camp life show that man does have a choice of action . . . . A [human] can preserve a vestige of spiritual freedom, of independence of mind, even in such conditions of psychic and spiritual duress."[49]

The openness of the future, both for ourselves and for God, challenges us to be creators of our own experience, taking responsibility for our moment-by-moment decisions as we seek to fulfill our role as God's companions in the ongoing evolution of the universe. Process theology suggests that the creative quest for beauty of experience may be a higher value than obedience or adherence to tradition, whether it involves our relationship with our government or the statutes of our faith tradition.

A Process-Relational God. While all talk about God must be framed in terms of the interplay of *kataphatic* and *apophatic* theology, that is, all things point to and reveal something of God, yet God is more than anything we can imagine, process theology asserts that our experience and understanding of God's nature and relationship with the world can be described in terms of the basic principles of process metaphysics: dynamic process, interdependence, creativity and freedom, and the universality of experience. According to Whitehead, "God is not to be treated as an exception to the metaphysical principles, invoked to save their collapse. He is their chief exemplification."[50] This statement undermines the absolute qualitative difference between God and the world prized by theologians such as Karl Barth and, thus, challenges traditional understandings of divine perfection, sovereignty, and worshipfulness. Process theologians suggest that God's relationship to the world is intimate and continuous rather than distant and discontinuous. God is not the "wholly other," but rather the "wholly present one," whose existence cannot be fully contained by the world. Without some degree of continuity between God and the world, divine love, relationship, and activity in the world are meaningless and irrelevant. This is the heart of process theology's *panentheistic* vision of "God in all things, and all things in God."

Perhaps, more scandalous to orthodox theologians is Whitehead's description of the relationship between God and creativity: "In all philosophic theory there is an ultimate which is actual in virtue of its accidents. It is only then capable of characterization through its accidental embodiments, and apart from these accidents is devoid of actuality. In the philosophy of organism this ultimate is termed 'creativity;' and God is its primordial, non-temporal accident."[51] This is a difficult concept to understand and accept. Some theologians otherwise well-disposed toward process theology, such as Robert Neville see God and creativity as one reality; God is both the impersonal ground of being and the personal creator and redeemer of all things.[52] This perception of the unity of God and creativity might have been at the heart of Bernard Loomer's belief that God contains both good and evil in the divine nature, and his recognition that Whitehead and others separated God and creativity primarily to preserve the unambiguous goodness of God. Other theologians suggest that Whitehead's distinction between God and creativity implies that there is a reality beyond God to which God is ontologically subservient.

In their understanding of the relationship of God and creativity, many process theologians, including myself, affirm that creativity is simply the ongoing movement or energy of the universe from which each creature's own self-creativity emerges. Creativity is not a separate reality standing behind the evolutionary process or God's existence, but the universal process of self-creation itself. As Whitehead notes, "it lies in the nature of things that the many enter into a complex unity."[53] Accordingly, Whitehead suggests that "creativity is the principle of novelty" by which each occasion, including God, shapes the data it experiences in a unique and unrepeatable fashion.[54] Creativity is the synergistic energy of process itself; in abstraction from God and the world of actual entities, creativity is without intentionality or purpose. Creativity neither precedes nor determines God's nature. Rather, there has always been a creative process, a world of finite entities, a realm of infinite possibility, and an infinitely relational and imaginative God, dynamically moving through all things in this universe from the first burst of energy described as the Big Bang to this present moment of experience. Creativity is the way things emerge in their process of self-creation, while God is the ever-creative source of order, meaning, and purpose within the process of creation. If such a situation were ever metaphysically possible: without God's primordial vision of possibility and dynamic and creative ordering of the universe through *initial aims*, or possibilities appropriate to each moment of experience, there would be only random chaos.

Whitehead's principle of creativity points to each occasion's self-creation. God's creative wisdom provides each occasion with the direction necessary for its creative process and the energy to aim at the highest good for itself and others. God cannot be separated from creativity, nor can creativity be separated from God. Yet, God, as the source of value and vision in the universe, cannot fully be identified entirely with *what is*, both good and evil; God aims for beauty and wholeness, or as Jesus said, abundant life, in all the movements of creative advance, both cosmic and microscopic. As Whitehead asserts, "the limitation of God is his goodness . . . . It is not true that God is in all respects infinite. If He were, He would be evil as well as good."[55]

Process theologians believe that an unequivocal identification of God with the creative energy of the universe would imply that God is the amoral source of both good and evil, and creation and destruction. God's power persuasively moves through the creative process, seeking good and evil, aiming at the well-being of the whole. A lively, interdependent, visionary, creative, and freely acting God integrates universality and intimacy in the ongoing cosmic adventure.

Concluding remarks. Process theology is breathtaking in its novelty, inclusiveness, and ability to shine new light on traditional Christian doctrines. In the chapters that follow, we will explore the significance of process theology for Christian faith. In each chapter, I will highlight the insights of various process theologians related to the chapter's particular theme in dialogue with my own interpretation of process theology and its relationship to Christian experience and practice.

CHAPTER 2

A TRULY PERSONAL GOD

A personal God is one who has social relations, really has them, and thus is constituted by relationships and hence is relative—in a sense not provided for by the traditional doctrine of a divine Substance wholly nonrelative toward the world, though allegedly containing loving relations between the "persons" of the Trinity.[1]

Old Testament scholar and process theologian Terence Fretheim asserts that "all too often the sole focus of the ministry of the church has been whether one believes in God. Insufficient attention has been given to the kind of God in which one believes, often with disastrous results."[2] Our beliefs about the relationship of God and the world, as I noted in the first chapter, can make the difference between life and death, spiritually, emotionally, and physically. Our beliefs can shape our attitudes toward global climate change, war and peace, persons of other religions, and marriage equality. According to Whitehead, "A religion, on its doctrinal side, can thus be defined as a system of general truths which have the effect of transforming character when they are sincerely held and vividly apprehended."[3] Further, Whitehead claims that "in the long run your character and your conduct of life depend on your intimate convictions."[4] This includes our intimate convictions about the nature of God's power, relationship with the world, the scope of salvation, and the meaning of revelation.[5] Accordingly, if we are to be theologically astute, we need to ask: Do our images of God promote what Whitehead described as "world loyalty" or do they encourage intolerance and sectarianism? Do our images of God encourage creativity or destruction? Do they inspire love or hatred? Are they defined primarily by loving partnership or by coercive power?

Recently, after the diagnosis of a rare form of cancer, a young man angrily confronted me with the admission, "I don't believe in God anymore after this. Why did God give me cancer? Wasn't it enough that God took away my mother when I was just nine years old?" On the other hand, I recall a college student giving thanks in a prayer meeting that she was not struck by the car that hit and killed another pedestrian on the same corner just a few minutes after she passed by. I appreciated her piety and sense of divine providence, but wondered how the deceased pedestrian's family and friends understood God's presence in the fatal accident. Did God somehow arbitrarily select her for survival, while choosing to end the life of an equally innocent bystander? Was this accident divinely planned or purely accidental?

Sadly, a good deal of Christian piety is grounded in the belief that God is the ultimate source of both illness and suffering, and good and evil. When a plane crashes, a tsunami hits, or an earthquake occurs, the first theological response invoked by many Christians is that the event was "God's will" or that "although it's a mystery to us, God has a plan with this tragedy." Even insurance companies speak of events that are out of our control, whether the failure of a car's braking system or the damage caused by a falling tree as "acts of God."

Worse yet, certain Christians believe that natural catastrophes as well as personal illness are the direct result of God's punishment of our sinful behavior. From this perspective, when we go astray from God's clearly articulated rules, God has every right to afflict us with AIDS, cancer, or natural disasters. For example, televangelist Pat Robertson asserted that the 2010 Haiti earthquake was the result of God's punishment of the Haitian people for a pact with the devil made nearly two centuries ago by Haitian freedom fighters. Many of us also remember Pat Roberson's and Jerry Falwell's blaming USA pro-choice policies and homosexuality for the events of September 11, 2001. Robertson also asserted that Katrina's devastation of New Orleans was the result of its acceptance of the homosexual lifestyle, even though, ironically, the tolerant and welcoming French Quarter of New Orleans was spared from significant damage while many conservative churches were destroyed. Megachurch pastor, John Piper, stated that an unexpected tornado that toppled the steeple of a Minnesota Lutheran church was God's warning to the Evangelical Lutheran Church in America for taking an affirmative position toward homosexuality at its 2010 General Assembly.

Such popular theologies credit God with behaviors that would lead to indictment or incarceration if they were committed by a parent. While a person can fear this punitive and mysterious God, process theology questions whether such a God can be truly loved or worshipped. In the words of John Cobb, "the God of traditional theism is dying and deserves to die."[6]

In the sections that follow, we will explore process theology's dynamic and relational vision of God through describing: (1) the main features of the traditional or classical doctrine of God, critiqued by process theology, (2) the characteristics of the living God of process theology, (3) process theology's response to the problem of evil, and (4) process theology's understanding of the relationship of prayer and divine activity. In particular, I will focus on the insights of Alfred North Whitehead, Charles Hartshorne, David Ray Griffin, and Marjorie Suchocki.

THE PROBLEM WITH PERFECTION

Changeless Perfection? Recently, in preparation for attending my fortieth high school reunion, I looked over the 1970 Year Book from James Lick High School in San Jose, California. While I didn't expect to find a good deal of theological reflection in the comments of seventeen year olds, one comment that I read several times struck me: "Bruce, to a great guy. Stay that way always." Now, what caught my attention was not just the allusion to my engaging personality, but the comment that I "stay that way always." I know that it was intended to be a compliment, but the notion that I would remain completely the same over forty years struck me as both humorous and impossible. In human life, growth is essential to well-being and maturity. Persons, institutions, or corporations that never change are labeled dysfunctional or irrelevant, and will likely, at least in the case of institutions and corporations, eventually cease to exist. Higher organisms, as Whitehead notes, "originate novelty to match the novelty of the environment."[7] In a world in which all things flow, ongoing creative transformation is not only healthy, but necessary for survival. Even Jesus underwent change and growth. As Luke 2:52 asserts, "Jesus grew in wisdom and stature and in divine and human favor." One gospel implies that Jesus learned an important lesson about God's love for the outsider from a Syrophonecian mother who came to him on behalf of her "demon possessed" daughter. (Mark 7:24–30)

In spite of the realities and benefits of growth and change in human existence, traditional Christian theology has typically identified perfection with changelessness, and change with inferiority, when it comes to describing God's nature. Divine perfection has been understood in terms of God's complete and unchanging awareness (omniscience) and absolute and unilateral power (omnipotence). Process theology takes a very different approach, affirming the primacy of love, transformation, and growth as essential to understanding of God's nature. But, in order to describe process theology's affirmation of a dynamic and relational God, we must first reflect on the nature of divine perfection as understood by the classical tradition in Christian theology. We will consider the classical vision of divine omniscience and omnipotence as examples of what process theologians describe as the problems of perfection.

At the heart of traditional Christian theology is the belief that God has unchanging knowledge of the universe, past, present, and future. Before the emergence of the universe, God had full awareness of all that would occur. Beyond time and space, God experiences the world at a single glance, viewing the entire expanse of creaturely experience in a timeless, unchanging eternal, now. Whether we describe God's awareness of the universe in terms of seeing a tapestry, a movie on DVD, or listening to music on a CD, classical theology described God as encompassing everything from beginning to end in one moment of experience.

In the emergence of Christian thought, the identification of perfection with God's unchanging omniscience reflects the influence of the Greek philosophers, Plato and Aristotle. According to Plato, the Forms are the unchanging and perfect models which the changing, decaying, and imperfect world imitates. The philosopher, or lover of wisdom, finds his or her true spiritual happiness and fulfillment in turning away from the ever-changing and shadowy world of bodies and emotions to the unchanging and eternal world of Forms. In fact, Plato's Socrates describes the body as a prison house, whose demands often stand in the way of our quest for the divine. Following his teacher Plato, Aristotle speaks of the ultimate cause of all things as the Unmoved or Prime Mover, which by its Pure Actuality attracts all things energetically toward itself. According to Aristotle, the ultimate cause of all things eternally and changelessly beholds itself in self-contained perfection. The Unmoved Mover is immune to change and is beyond the vagaries of embodied existence. If the Unmoved

Mover were to undergo change or experience our world of birth and decay, it would move from perfection to imperfection, and better to worse. Divine perfection is incompatible with experiencing our changing world in its decay, conflict, joy, and challenge. Aristotle asserts that the Cause of all things "is thinking of that which is most divine and honorable, and He is not changing; for change would be for the worse, and change would be a motion."[8] Clearly, God cannot be thinking of us, for, our passions and projects could only sully divine perfection!

Grounded in the identification of perfection with disembodied and unchanging existence, traditional types of spiritual formation, beginning with Plato's *Phaedo* and throughout the Christian mystical tradition, aim at drawing us away from the distractions of physical existence. Our goal is, in the spirit of Plotinus and his Christian followers, the spiritual movement from multiplicity, to unity, and flesh to spirit, thus, finding our true home in eternal, unchanging, and disembodied existence.

Christian theology has struggled for two thousand years to integrate the vision of the living, active, creative, and historically involved God, celebrated by the Hebraic tradition, the incarnation of Jesus as the word made flesh who suffered at Calvary, and the unchanging and impassive reality of Aristotle's Unmoved Mover. Theologically, this has been a challenging enterprise. While the everyday religious experience of pastors and their congregants centers around practicing intercessory prayer and seeking to follow Jesus' mandate to create a world in time and space reflective of God's heavenly vision of Shalom, the God to whom people often pray and worship was often understood as determining everything in advance and oblivious to our intercessory prayers. The pain Jesus experienced on the cross was often placed in contrast to the divine apathy, suggested by the Greek vision of unchanging perfection, which by definition was immune to the suffering that Jesus experienced.

Traditional understandings of divine omniscience affirm that God knows everything in advance. Such theologies can be comforting to believers. Recently, a friend wrote to me telling of his wife's diagnosis with life-threatening cancer. Amid his pain, he wrote that he felt secure, for "God is in control, and God's plan is always good." He took consolation in the fact that nothing can surprise God and, in principle, God holds the future as well as the past in God's eternal self-awareness. While I honor his faith and confidence in divine foreknowledge and control of the events of our lives, such religious comfort is bought at a great price, theologically speaking. If God knows everything in advance, then past, present, and future have already been determined. All the days of our lives from conception to death have been written, and determined, by God in eternity; we just don't know it. There is nothing new we can add or contribute to God's experience or enjoyment of the universe. Accordingly, our experience of creativity and freedom are ultimately a sham, since all of our actions are already known and, by implication, decided by God. Further, what we perceive as negative—tsunami, earthquake, automobile accident, and cancer—is ultimately good because it is part of God's eternal plan.

From this perspective, divine awareness of our world and our lives is always observational rather than personal. Jesus' sense of God's abandonment on the cross is not surprising; what else could he expect from a distant and apathetic Parent? More than that, if the cross and resurrection were already known in advance, Jesus' suffering was charade both for God and, perhaps, for Jesus himself. If God's experience of our pain and joy is predetermined, detached, and unemotional, then truly we are God-forsaken in our moments of deepest need.

As we shall see later in this chapter, the practice of prayer is intimately related to our belief that the future is, to some extent, open and can be altered by our prayers. Process theologians suggest that traditional understandings of divine knowledge and power as complete and unchanging, render the practice of prayer a meaningless activity. If everything is known by God in advance, then prayer alters nothing for us, the lives of others, or God's experience of the world. Further, if the events of the world unilaterally and fully reflect God's will, there is nothing we can do to change the present or future by prayer or social action. We pray for our sake alone; our prayers can change nothing in the already known and predetermined world of time and space. The practice of prayer is rendered superfluous insofar as it contributes nothing of value to God or others' lives.

Process theologians also reflect on the problems of perfection, grounded in the classical image of divine immutability, when it comes to understanding God's own experience of the world. A God who knows everything in advance cannot change, grow, and do new things. While nothing surprises the God of traditional theism, the eternal and changeless deity, ironically, is imprisoned by its eternal self-awareness. While we perceive ourselves, perhaps falsely, according to traditional theology, doing new things and growing spiritually and relationally, God can neither experience nor do anything new. God cannot add or subtract to the narrative that God has already written. In fact, similar to the film "Groundhog Day," in which the protagonist experiences the same day repeated over and over again, God must live with same "world at a glance" without respite or novelty. In many ways, process theologians suggest, the God of unchanging and eternal knowledge is far less interesting and creative than the average mortal who must adapt, even if imperfectly, to surprising events throughout the day. Further, an unchanging and apathetic God is unable to fully love the world God has created in ways that are congruent with the vision of healthy parenting described by Jesus in the parables and the Lord's Prayer.

More than this, the God who knows everything, changelessly in advance is unable to have meaningful relationships with the changing world. God cannot empathize with Jesus' suffering on the cross or our own personal challenges. The philosopher Anselm stated the problems of divine perfection as clearly and unabashedly as any theologian in history.

> If thou art passionless, thou dost not feel sympathy; and if thou dost not feel sympathy, thy heart is not wretched from sympathy for the wretched; but this is what it is to be compassionate. But if thou art not compassionate, where cometh such great consolation to the wretched? . . . Truly, thou art compassionate in terms of our experience, but art not so in terms of thine own. For, when thou beholdest us in our wretchedness, we experience the effect of compassion, but thou dost not experience the feeling. Therefore, thou art both compassionate, because thou dost save the wretched, and spare those who sin against thee; and not compassionate, because thou art affected by no sympathy for wretchedness.[9]

An impassive, unchanging God goes through the motions of loving us, but cannot feel our pain or joy. This a far cry from the intimacy of Jesus' vision of God as "Abba" or "Daddy." Process theologians believe that authentic healthy human and divine love is relational, sympathetic, and attentive to the joys as well as the sorrows of the beloved. Relational love takes the beloved so seriously that it willingly embraces her or his experience as part of one's own, allowing the lover to be shaped by the beloved's feelings, priorities, and values.

While deeply-committed love is constant in its care, it is also constantly adapting to the needs and experience of our beloved. In fact, care without mutuality and empathy is a "one way street" that leads to the objectification of the beloved. Sadly, as process theologians note, traditional understandings of divine experience imply that God is less sympathetic, loving, and responsive then we are. In this spirit, open and relational theologian, Thomas Oord comments, "love requires relational philosophy. We cannot understand love well when we ignore relationality."[10]

When theologians join timeless divine omniscience with the traditional doctrine of omnipotence, defined as having exerting or possessing complete power to determine all things, they ultimately must also admit, as process theologians assert, that good and evil must equally be attributed to God. Process theologians further note that traditional images of divine sovereignty understand God's power as unilateral and unidirectional. God gives, but does not receive. God calls, but does not respond. God commands, but does not listen. In human life, such unilateral relationships are often identified by psychologists with parental narcissism and emotional neglect.

Whitehead suggests that traditional Christian theology took a tragic turn when it chose Caesar over Jesus, eternity over time, and power over love.

The notion of God as the "unmoved mover" is derived from Aristotle, at least as far as Western thought is concerned. The notion of God as "eminently real" is a favorite doctrine of Christian theology. The combination of the two into the doctrine of an aboriginal, eminently real, transcendent creator, at whose fiat the world came into being, and whose imposed will it obeys, is the fallacy that has infused tragedy into the histories of Christianity and Mohametism [Islam]. When the Western world accepted Christianity, Caesar conquered . . . . The brief Galilean vision of humility flickered throughout the ages, uncertainly. In the official formulation of the religion, it has assumed the trivial form of the mere attribution to the Jews that they cherished a misconception about their Messiah. But the deeper idolatry, of the fashioning of God in the image of the Egyptian, Persian, and Roman imperial rulers, was retained. The church gave unto God the attributes which belonged exclusively to Caesar.[11]

In noting the neglect of healthy relatedness and love in Christian theology, Thomas Oord asserts that while the role of sovereignty, faith, and the church are important in theological reflection, "when considered *the* center of formal or systematic theology, these matters have drawn Christians away from a coherent understanding of God's love and the love God calls creatures to express. Too often, placing other concerns as theology's orienting concern results in Christian dogma inconsistent with love."[12] When it comes to theological reflection, process theology follows the Apostle Paul's affirmation that "the greatest of these is love." (I Corinthians 13:13)

The Problems and Ironies of Omnipotence. As a practical theologian, whose work joins teaching, preaching, and pastoral care, I am especially concerned with the lived meaning of theological doctrines. When we consider the nature of divine omnipotence, as traditionally understood, we need to ask questions such as: What does it mean to say God is all-powerful? Or, that God is "in control" as some evangelical Christian say? Theologians and believers alike have equivocated in terms of describing the extent of God's power. Nevertheless, apart from the extreme punitive-oriented, rewards-punishments positions of Falwell and Robertson, traditional doctrines of omnipotence beg the following questions asked by layperson and pastor alike:

- Does God intentionally cause natural catastrophes such as the Christmas tsunami, Hurricane Katrina, or the 2010 Haiti earthquake?
- Does God intentionally cause cancer, birth defects, and chronic illness?
- Does God choose who lives and who dies in the case of an airplane crash, car accident, or falling structure?
- Does God determine who will believe in Jesus as savior and who will not, thus sealing the eternal destiny of human beings before they're even born?
- Does God determine our life span to the exact date of our deaths?
- Is God ultimately the source of childhood sexual abuse, rape, incest, and domestic violence?
- Does God fully determine the future such that our efforts to protect the earth are of no value whatsoever?
- Does God permit such evils to occur as a way of testing or strengthening us?

If you answer "no" to any of these questions, then, to some extent, the traditional doctrines of divine omniscience and omnipotence have become theologically problematic for you. While it is clear that divine omnipotence, reflected in the doctrine of predestination, has been a source of comfort to the faithful in times of persecution and doubt, the doctrine of divine omnipotence can also lead to a clear distinction among believers between the "saved" and "unsaved." It can also shape how the "saved" view their ethical responsibilities in relationship to those who are excluded from God's grace before the creation of the world. After all, the infidel and heathen have no rights whatsoever in relationship to the "manifest destiny" of God's chosen ones; if they are objects of God's wrath, they are ultimately unworthy of our care and moral consideration. Further, although some would say that pot has no right to question the potter who is responsible for its very existence, such comments assume that God can do anything God wants to creation without regard to the well-being of individual creatures. (Romans 9:21) This is not love, but narcissism and objectification, according to process theologians.

Ironically, when changeless omniscience and absolute omnipotence are combined, God's creativity and freedom as well as love are compromised. Just as the vision of divine perfection in terms of unchanging omniscience leads to descriptions of God's experience as less interesting and inventive than God's ever-changing creatures, an unchanging all-powerful God is, by definition, limited and competitive with the creaturely world. If God determines all that will occur in advance, then God cannot exercise power in novel and creative ways. Everything has already been decided, including God's ability to be innovative. The ongoing exercise of divine power is limited by what God has already determined; God can't change God's previous decisions or inject new possibilities into the historical process. This viewpoint, of course, is countered by the lively, historically-involved image of God, described in the Hebrew Scriptures and process theology.

Although traditional theology affirms God's absolute power, some traditional theologians still suggest the possibility of creaturely agency in the realm of this-worldly interactions. This doctrine, however, creates more problems than it solves in light of the relationship of divine and creaturely power. If all is determined in advance, then there is only a finite amount of divine or creaturely agency to go around. By definition, this leads to a zero sum understanding of the relationship of God and humankind. In game theory and economics, zero sum games are "win-lose" in orientation: if I gain, you lose, whether in terms of resources, power, or chess pieces. In theology, this means that any creaturely agency or creativity robs God of sovereignty, majesty, or power. From this perspective, divine grace is unilateral; we can do absolutely nothing good apart from grace. Anything humans do through their own initiative is flawed or disobedient. A humorous example of this type of theology is reflected in a conversation I had with a third year seminary student: after I complemented a seminarian on the quality of her sermon, she responded with "Oh, it wasn't me. God did everything today." To which I replied, "I thought I saw you preaching, and not God, today!" In relationship to the all-powerful and all-determining God, the only possible response is subservience or passivity. Yet, once again, ironically, many persons who believed in divine predestination also assumed that they were God's instruments in civilizing native persons, whether in Africa, Australia, or the Americas, and that God blessed their economic success at the expense of those whom God had chosen not to bless. Their victory, prosperity, and political domination were sure signs of divine election just as the defeat of aboriginal people revealed the God-forsakenness of the continent's earliest inhabitants.

In contrast, process theology affirms an ever-growing, open-source understanding of power in which the call and response of divine and human creativity leads to greater expressions of power in the relationships among the creator and the creatures. Process theologians assert that when Jesus promised his followers that they would do "greater things" in the future (John 14:12), he invited them to be creative, adventurous, and inventive in ways that add to God's glory and contribute to God's evolving enjoyment of the universe. The more creative we are, the more creative God can be; the more creative God is, the more creative creatures can be in response.

A Purpose Driven or Adventurous God? Although it is unusual to include the work of popular preachers and best-selling authors in serious theological texts, I believe that theological accessibility requires us to take the insights of popular theologians seriously. Televangelists and authors such as Jerry Falwell, Joel Osteen, Pat Robertson, T.D. Jakes, Max Lucado, Robert Schuller, and Joyce Meyer, to name a few, have had more direct influence in shaping North American and global religious reflection than seminary professors and, accordingly, must be taken seriously by anyone who affirms alternative understandings of God's nature and activity. In fact, their voices are typically the only theologically-oriented voices heard in the public religious square. Almost to a person, their theology often reflects traditional images of God as omnipotent, omniscient, and punitive, without serious reflection or questioning. If process theology is to be a guide to today's perplexed Christians and seekers, it must be willing to address directly the insights and oversights of best-selling texts by popular theologians and televangelists. In this spirit, I am contrasting the theological vision of process theology with that of Rick Warren, currently the most influential popular theologian in the USA and across the globe.

As we discovered in the first chapter, Rick Warren, author of the best-selling *The Purpose Driven Life*, is an example of the strengths and weaknesses of traditional theology, played out on the stage of popular theology. Warren's Orange County, California based message is directed toward persons who have everything in life except a sense of meaning, that is, persons whose affluence enables them to acquire everything except peace of mind. Warren promises that taking the forty day spiritual journey that he proposes will enable persons to "know God's purpose for your life and [you] will understand the big picture—how all the pieces of your life fit together. Having this perspective will reduce your stress, simplify your decisions, increase your satisfaction, and, most important, prepare you for eternity."[13]

Warren unabashedly affirms that God is in control of everything from the molecules in our bodies to the future of planet Earth. Following the traditional integration of omniscience and omnipotence, Warren asserts that "His purpose for your life predates your conception. He planned it before you existed, *without your input.*"[14] Warren elaborates that "God prescribed every single detail of your body. He deliberately chose your race, the color of your skin, your hair, and every other feature. He custom-made your body just the way he wanted it. He also determined the natural talents you would possess and the uniqueness of your personality."[15] God does everything for a reason, including choosing our parents. "It doesn't matter whether your parents were good or bad, or indifferent. God knew that those two individuals possessed *exactly* the right genetic make up to create a custom 'you' he had in mind."[16] From Warren's perspective, it's clearly all about God: God is the potter, we are the clay. Our joy and sorrow matters little in light of God's plan for the universe.

God's way will always prevail regardless of its impact on the life of the creature.

Not everyone however buys Warren's traditional understanding of divine decision-making. After reading the first few chapters of Warren's book, a woman who had experienced physical abuse as a child protested, "Warren says it doesn't matter whether your parents were good or bad! Well, I beg to differ. My parents were alcoholics who beat my sisters and me. It's taken me years to deal with this. I can't believe that God would approve, or plan, child abuse!" The parents of a child born with spina bifida countered Warren's theological position, "We love our son with all our heart and thank God for him every day, but if God planned our son's spina bifida and the pain he's experienced just to test him and us, God's no better than the devil!"

God constantly tests us, Warren observes, in order to observe how we'll respond.[17] Such a theological affirmation begs the questions: Does this mean that God was testing the Haitian people with the 2010 earthquake? Or, that God was testing a child born with fetal alcohol syndrome as a result of her mother's substance abuse? Or, that the teenage children of a mother diagnosed with terminal cancer are somehow being evaluated on how this event will shape the rest of their lives and their sense of God's love for them? After reflecting on this particular section of the *Purpose Driven Life,* one reader noted that "it sounds that we're no more than lab rats, part of a divine experiment, in which our success or failure doesn't affect the experimenter."

Warren, however, is unrelenting in drawing the necessary conclusions of the traditional doctrines of divine omnipotence and omniscience. He affirms that "God has a purpose behind every problem." Warren continues, "regardless of the cause, none of your problems could happen without God's permission. Everything that happens is *Father-filtered* and he intends to use it for good even when Satan and others mean it for bad."[18] God ultimately chooses everything that happens to us, "God's plan for your life involves all that happens to you—including your mistakes, your sins, and your hurts. This includes illness, debt, disasters, divorce, and death of loved ones."[19] Warren believes that all things work together for good for those who love God and are called into God's realm. (Romans 8:28—29) This is good news for the chosen and faithful, and for those who feel certain of their salvation. It is, however, bad news for those who lie outside the boundaries of grace or who are beaten down by the circumstances of life. For the wayward, "all things work together for *bad.*"[20] From Warren's perspective, the only way a person can find meaning in this life and companionship with God in eternity is to color inside the lines that God has already drawn and perform her or his role entirely as God has written it. Warren's unrelenting affirmation of divine power led one layperson to refer sarcastically to his book as "the puppet driven life!"

Although Warren speaks of God as loving, it is clear that Warren subordinates love to sovereignty in his understanding of God's character and relationship to the world. Caesar rather than Jesus characterizes Warren's understanding of God's relationship to humankind. As benevolent as Warren's God is to the faithful, those who fail at life's tests of faith are lost in this life and eternity, despite the fact that their failure is ultimately God's doing; God intentionally creates the challenges that lead them astray or overwhelm their coping abilities. Warren's God falls under Charles Hartshorne's critique of traditional images of God: "Theologies have never taken really the proposition that God is love."[21]

In contrast, process theology affirms an open source, adventurous, and constantly evolving universe in which God and creatures are constantly doing new things. As we will see in the following sections, God and humankind are partners in synergistic ways that give new meaning to the power of prayer and our response to the problem of suffering and evil. Rather than planning all the important events of our lives and then testing our responses to adversity, process theology sees God as the Holy Adventurer who invites us to be companions on our own holy adventures.[22] While God challenges us to greater creativity and adventure, God never gives up on anyone, nor is God directly responsible for our pain and suffering.

GOD AS INTIMATE COMPANION

John Cobb and David Ray Griffin describe God in terms of "creative-responsive love."[23] Whereas traditional visions of God assert that God is ultimately independent of the world, giving but not receiving, determining every event in advance, process theology affirms, in contrast, that God is intimately related to each moment of experience, giving and receiving love, and touching and being touched by the joys and sorrows of the world. Philosopher Charles Hartshorne states that "God orders the universe, according to panentheism, by taking into his own life all the currents of feeling in existence. He is the most irresistible of experiences because he himself is the most open to influence."[24] In this statement Hartshorne introduces a technical term, unfamiliar to many readers, *panentheism*. Panentheism affirms that God is present in all things and, conversely, that all things are present in God. God is "more" than the world, but also intimately in touch with all things, shaping and being shaped by each moment of experience. The living God joins the eternal and the temporal, and possibility and actuality, in the ongoing evolution of the universe.

The Power of Possibility. Although virtually all Christian theology describes God as creator or creative principle of the world, descriptions of the nature, scope, and extent of divine creativity vary among theologians. Traditional theology often understands divine creativity as unilateral and all-determining. It asserts that God creates the world "in the beginning" out of nothing. Everything that occurs ultimately depends upon God's providential and predestined activity such that each moment and the whole span of history reflect God's will for it. Process theology takes a very different approach to the relationship of divine and creaturely agency and power. According to Whitehead, the limitation of God is God's goodness.[25] God does not cause all things, but creates *in, through,* and *with* all things. Divine power, accordingly, is relational rather than coercive in nature. God's power is the power of an ideal, a vision that lures each moment of experience toward what it can become in light of its environmental context.

Whitehead uses the term *initial aim* to describe God's influence on each occasion of experience. According to Whitehead, each occasion of experience "derives from God its basic conceptual [initial] aim, relevant to its actual world, yet with indeterminations awaiting its actual decisions."[26] Further, Whitehead asserts that the "initial stage of its [each occasion of experience] aim is rooted in the nature of God, and its completion depends on the self-causation of the subject-superject."[27] As the source of the initial aim, God not only guides the evolving order of the universe, but also brings forth new possibilities in our lives and in the cosmic adventure. According to process theologians, faithfulness to God calls us to cherish the past as well as to embrace the present in the context of God's visions for the future, be it the next moment or the horizon of history. More than that, God is the restless source of possibility, urging the universe at every level, toward greater levels of complexity and intensity of experience. The Divine Eros not only presents us moment by moment with new possibilities, but also gives us the energy and desire to realize these possibilities in our personal and community lives.

In describing the relationship between divine possibility and creaturely decision making, Whitehead notes that the quality and intensity of God's influence on the world is limited by our past history, including our choices. Although God constantly aims at abundant life and beauty of experience, God's presentation to each occasion of its highest possibilities for self-creation, that is, its initial aim "is the best for that *impasse.* But, if the best be bad, then the ruthlessness of God can be personified as *Ate,* the goddess of mischief. The chaff is burnt."[28] To many readers, this is a challenging passage insofar as it seems to identify God with some of the evils we experience. I believe this passage suggests that God's power is always personal and contextual, working in our lives *as they are* in terms of what they *can be.* God's impact on a particular moment of experience is congruent with naturalistic causal relationships rather than being an abstract supernatural intervention. In a particular concrete moment of experience, for example, given my previous decisions, God's highest aim may not explicitly aim at self-transcending love toward the stranger, but that I refrain from yelling at the driver of the car who cuts in front of me or that after I have had "one too many" at a local pub, I choose to take a cab rather than drive home. Or, if a person has suffered abuse or humiliation at the hands of others, God's vision of healing may not immediately include forgiveness or letting go of the hurt, but anger and confrontation, as reflective the first small steps toward self-affirmation. In another situation, God's vision may be for a person's gentle and peaceful death, after she has said "good bye" to her family, when a physical cure is not possible even for God. Even in the realm of joining possibility with actuality, God does not act unilaterally or abstractly, but by presenting each moment with a vision of the best possible outcomes, or array of possibilities, and the energy to embody God's ideal on its own terms. God's power is revealed in love and persuasion and not domination.

Process theology sees Jesus' ministry as the prime example of divine persuasion. Although Jesus constantly confronted people with God's vision of Shalom and radical hospitality, Jesus seldom transformed people's lives apart from their consent. In conversation with a man who was paralyzed for nearly four decades, Jesus asks, "do you want to be made well?" (John 5:6) To a sight impaired man, Jesus questions, "what do you want me to do for you?" (Mark 10:50) Jesus called people to decision—he did not coerce people to join him as companions in God's coming realm.

God is present seeking value and intensity of experience in every moment of our lives, not just in human experience but in every momentary occasion of experience from quantum particles to cats and angels. In more poetic language, Whitehead describes God's love for the world as "the particular providence for particular occasions."[29]

Still, every moment of experience, whether human or non-human, freely responds to God's vision for it in light of its own creative process. We can choose to follow God's vision for the present moment and the immediate future, or we can turn away from God's ideal for us and focus solely on our own individual well-being. While creaturely freedom and creativity are variable, they are nevertheless universal, whether at the human, non-human, and cellular levels.

We may creatively choose to embody positive ideals that go in a different direction than God's ideal for the moment. In the open system universe, our creativity and freedom is not necessarily a fall from grace, even when it diverges from God's vision, but an adventure in action and imagination that enables God and us to do new things. Although God's primordial vision is intimate and global, and embraces infinite possibilities, process theology suggests that God can be imagined as an intimate, creative, and freedom supporting parent, who says to her child, "Surprise me, do something I hadn't fully expected, so that together we can bring about something new and exciting." Grace abounds in the world and in our lives, according to process theology, encouraging rather than condemning creaturely initiative. God wants us to do new things and shape the grace we have received in accordance with our own self-determination.

Process theology asserts that we experience God *with* the world and not apart from our everyday life. God presents each moment's ideal possibilities in the context of our experience of our immediate world, including the past moment of experience, our overall health and well-being, the environment, and previous embodiments of the divine call and human response. God never gives up on anyone or anything. The initial aim testifies to the universality of revelation, from which, on occasion, unique and intense experiences of divine guidance and power may emerge. These often unexpected mystical moments or life-changing experiences occur as a result of the interplay of divine call and human response. The ongoing choice to be attentive to God's aim through spiritual practices enables us to more fully experience God's vision for our lives in the moment as well as in the context of a lifetime.

Process theology's understanding of God's presence in our lives in terms of the initial aim joins the insights of the otherwise conflicting Augustinian and Lutheran with the Pelagian and Wesleyan visions of Christianity. With Luther and Augustine, process theology affirms that God's grace is always prior to our personal response and comes to us by God's initiative, regardless of our previous lives. Divine possibility inspires and energizes each moment of experience. Grace is not contingent on our goodness or achievement. God never gives up on any creature, giving it life and hope in every moment of experience. We grow in grace because God is graceful to us. In the spirit of John Wesley and the much misunderstood and maligned Pelagius, process theology also affirms that God's graceful presence calls for a human response which brings us closer or further away from God's ideal for our lives and conditions God's future movements in our lives. Grace and freedom are neither absolute nor antagonistic in relationship to one another, but are inter dependent in the ongoing call and response of God and the world. As Whitehead notes in *Religion in the Making*, "every act leaves the world with a deeper or fainter impress of God. He then passes into his next relation to the world with enlarged or diminished presentations of ideals."[30] God constantly responds to us personally and intimately in terms of our life history and previous decisions.

Process theology affirms that divine power is relational and persuasive, not all-determining. Traditional understandings of divine power as all-determining are incompatible with the dual affirmations of creaturely creativity and divine goodness. This is among the most controversial aspects of process theology, one which renders it unacceptable to many "orthodox" Christians who see absolute and unfettered power as essential to divine sovereignty and human worship. In contrast, process theologians affirm that although God cannot, and does not, do everything, a constantly creative God is ultimately infinite in power and creativity, that is, there is no limitation, other than God's loving care, to the unfolding of God's power in the ongoing evolution of the universe. God's goodness and love, not power, are the ground of worship and obedience. God does not cause the cancer, nor could God have ultimately prevented the occurrence of cancer, an earthquake in Haiti, or a flood in Pakistan. But, God is present as a force promoting healing, compassion, and strength amid the pain. God is not limited by God's past decisions, but can bring forth new possibilities in light of creaturely decisions.

Whitehead affirms that the teleology, or aim, of the universe is directed toward the realization of beauty.[31] The universe is the theatre of divine artistry and glory, but unlike the Calvinist tradition, God's glory embraces all creation, seeking wholeness for every creature in its particular environmental context. God plays no favorites, but seeks abundant life for all creatures. The universality of God's initial aim, or vision of possibilities for each creature, reflects God's delight in all creation and God's love for each creature. No one is left behind or forgotten in a world in which God patiently seeks the salvation of all things.

The Fellow Sufferer Who Understands. Just as controversial in light of traditional doctrines of divine perfection is process theology's affirmation that the world contributes to and shapes God's experience. Rather than turning inward in narcissistic self-absorption, process theology asserts that God is completely oriented toward the world. God embraces every moment of experience intimately, feeling its joy and sorrow, and responding with new and life-giving possibilities. Alfred North Whitehead's description of divine compassion bounds on poetry, no doubt reflecting Whitehead's philosophical quest for a reality that gives everlasting significance to the constantly-changing world, including the lives of those, like his son Eric, who die prematurely.

> The wisdom of [God's] subjective aim prehends [experiences] every actuality for what it can be in a perfected system—its sufferings, its sorrows, its failures, its triumphs, its immediacies of joy—woven by rightness of feeling into the harmony of the universal feeling, which is always immediate, always many, always one, moving onward and never perishing . . . . The image—and it is but an image—the image under which this operative growth of God's nature is best conceived, is that of a tender care that nothing be lost.[32]

We may forget, but God never forgets. Although God experiences all things that occur within what Whitehead describes as the *consequent nature*, God's experience of the unfolding of the universe in space and time is holistic and value-laden as well as objective. God sees everything as it is, but also everything as it could be in light of God's vision of Shalom and beauty. The integration of God's primordial and infinite vision of possibility, or *primordial nature*, and God's consequent experience of the world is guided by God's quest for beauty and creative transformation, both for God and for the world. God sees creation through the eyes of love. As Whitehead affirms, God "saves the world as it passes into the immediacy of his own life. It is the judgment of a tenderness which loses nothing that can be saved. It is also the judgment of a wisdom which uses what in the temporal world is mere wreckage."[33]

Process theology affirms that God embraces our joy and suffering and that God's experience of the world "grows" in relationship to the ongoing universe. Divine omniscience is not defined as knowledge of everything that will happen in the future, but the embrace of everything that happens in the universe moment by moment in real, ongoing time. God's experience embraces the eternal and temporal, and abstract and concrete. The source of all possibility, God also moves within and is shaped by the dynamic interdependence of the temporal world. Divine activity is within time in terms of God's concrete experience and action in the evolving universe, and beyond time in terms of God's vision of possibilities for all things. God's uniqueness is God's ability embrace of the world in its entirety, moment by moment, in real time. For process theologians, the timelessness cherished by traditional theology is an abstraction and not a theological virtue. In contrast, process theologians believe that timelessness finds its fulfillment in God's creative-responsive love in the temporal world.

Divine omniscience, according to process theologians, does not entail a timeless vision of the future in its actuality. Rather, God knows the actual completely as actual, while embracing future possibilities as potentialities, not settled events. New things happen to God; God has new experiences. The immediacy and universality of divine omniscience evolving in relationship to the world enables God to respond intimately to each creature in its context. Accordingly, while God persists as the source of possibility and order through all changes, God also is shaped by all changes. God is adventurous, too. God does not fully know what the outcome of any event or encounter will be in its entirety until it occurs, but God has the resources, the "particular providence for particular occasions," to creatively and lovingly respond to each contingency in the ongoing universe.

For process theologians, God's ability to shape our world is intimately related to God's embrace of the world as it is. Divine perfection, accordingly, involves God's ability not only to influence all things, but to be the "most moved mover," influenced by all things. As Charles Hartshorne asserts, "everything that influences God has already been influenced by God."[34] God is unsurpassable, although God constantly surpasses and grows as a result of God's previous and current experiences.

Traditional theologies have often implied that God did not fully experience Jesus' suffering on the cross except in terms of timeless observation. From the perspective of divine impassibility, *partipassianism,* or the belief that "the Father suffers," was considered a heresy insofar as it suggested the whole of the Trinity experienced Jesus' pain and that the immutable God was touched by creaturely suffering and mortality. Divine perfection excluded everything but an abstract, pre-determined, and observational relationship to Jesus' suffering on the cross. In contrast, process theologians assert that God was in Christ reconciling the world by experiencing Jesus' pain as God's own pain. The Cross of Jesus witnesses to God's actual experiences of pain and joy, and not to a previously written script, in which God observes but does not truly feel Jesus' anguish. In the dance of the Trinity, God fully experiences the pain of the world, including Jesus' death on the cross. Like the most loving of parents, God feels the pain and rejoices in the beauty of all creation from the inside as well as in terms of the impact of our actions. In the words of William Blake:

> Can I see another's woe,
> And not be in sorrow, too?
> Can I see another's grief,
> And not seek for kind relief?
> Can I see a falling tear,
> And not feel my sorrows share?
> Can a father see his child
> Weep, nor be with sorrow filled?
> Can a mother sit and hear
> An infant groan, an infant fear.
> No, no! Never can it be!

Never, never can it be.
And can he who smiles on all
Hear the wren with sorrows small,
Hear the small bird's grief and care,
Hear the woes that infants bear,
And not sit beside the nest,
Pouring pity on the breast,
And not sit the cradle near,
Wiping tear on infant's fear;
And not sit both night & day,
Wiping all our tears away.
O! Never can it be!
Never can it be!
He doth give his joy to all;
He becomes the infant small;
He becomes a man of woe;
He doth feel the sorrow too.
Think thou canst sigh a sigh;
And thy maker is not by;
Think not thou canst wipe a tear,
And thy maker is not near.
O! He gives to us his joy
That our grief he may destroy;
Till our grief is fled and gone
He doth sit by us and moan.[35]

The dynamic, living God is truly with us. The One to whom all hearts are open, and all desires known, knows and treasures our lives, preserving them everlastingly in God's all-inclusive experience. God seeks beauty and love relentlessly for us, even when we turn away as persons and communities. Through all the changes of life, God truly is "the poet of the world, with tender patience leading it by his vision of truth, beauty, and love."[36]

DIVINE POWER AND CREATURELY SUFFERING

Process theologians assert that traditional notions of God as all-knowing, in terms of including knowledge of future events in their entirety, and all-determining, as the ultimate cause of all that happens, make God equally the source of evil and good and render God's actions amoral and arbitrary in relationship to the created world. Or, to put it another way, traditional understandings of divine power assert that nothing happens apart from divine determination or permission, even that which appears to be contrary to God's will for humankind and the world.

Some theologians such as Martin Luther and John Calvin unabashedly deny any form of creaturely agency altogether and attribute what we judge to be good and evil equally to God. According to Luther, "God foreknows nothing contingently, but that He foresees, purposes, and does all things according to His own immutable, eternal, and infallible will."[37] As creatures, God owes us nothing, not even love, as a result of our sinfulness and creaturely status, and can harden our hearts or lead us to damnation without consideration to any intentions or experiences we might have. Calvin continues this same chain of reasoning with his unapologetic affirmation that "not one drop of rain falls without God's command" and that God determines "when a branch breaking off from a tree kills a passing traveler."[38] While divine predestination is consolation to the elect, or saved, whose salvation is eternally chosen by God, those whom God has overlooked or defined as reprobate, are "damned if they do and damned if they don't." In line with Augustine, Aquinas, Luther, and Calvin, proponents of traditional understandings of divine power sacrifice God's love and goodness before the altar of sovereign power.

In contrast, process theology affirms a relational understanding of power in which God works *with* the world, providing ideals and the energy to embody them, rather than unilaterally determining everything that occurs. Although the potential expressions of God's presence and power are infinite, God's relational power is always contextual, personal, concrete, and finite in terms of each moment of experience. God is the highest example of the morality toward which we aspire, rather than an exception to our quest for Shalom or abundant life for ourselves and the world. Creaturely choice and agency are real and cherished by God. Accordingly, as David Ray Griffin notes, "it is impossible for God to have a monopoly on power" in a universe in which existence implies some level of self-determination.[39] Although God is the source of the initial aim, God's aim is given as formative data along with the rest of the universe from which each moment's experience arises, and is integrated in accordance with each moment's decision-making process. While the simplest creatures almost always reflect the divine aim in their process of self-creation, some simple entities deviate from the divine aim, for example, cancer cells and genetic abnormalities. God does not cause cells to become cancerous but influences them toward health and order in light of the impact of both environmental and genetic factors. God is never the only cause but one of many causes for each moment of experience. Still, as I stated earlier in this chapter, creaturely choices, both positive and negative, do not compete with God's infinite resourcefulness, but enable God to provide new possibilities for growth, creativity, and healing.

Process theologians affirm the essential goodness of God, noting with Whitehead that teleology of the universe is aimed at beauty of experience, involving the interplay of complexity, contrast, and intensity of experience. God's quest for beauty, however, always occurs in the context of the evolving universe of self-determining creatures. In using the word "evolving," I am explicitly affirming that God is the organ of both order and novelty, and tradition and innovation, in the course of the multi-billion year evolutionary process. God has always been creating, and the universe has always been in process, from the first moments of the big bang to the emergence of 100 billion galaxies over the past fourteen billion years. Like an artist, God has created out of the welter of materials available, bringing cosmic order out of what would have been chaos and then bringing forth level upon level of complexity in our galaxy and billions of others. In describing the universe-creating process, David Ray Griffin asserts that "the creation of our world is understandable as a process of bringing order out of a state of absolute or near absolute chaos."[40] What would have been random and, for all intents and purposes, insentient has evolved into a world supporting complex organisms, able to create as well to destroy, to celebrate as well as to suffer, and to love as well as to hate. In a less complex universe, there would have been less freedom, agency, and imagination, and also less pain. In bringing forth a universe of highly sensitive and creative organisms, God has set the stage for both ugliness and beauty as a result of creaturely choices.

Process theologians note that with greater the complexity of experience, there is also greater possibility for moral evil as well as physical and emotional pain. Yet, greater freedom also means greater value for oneself and the future. While God does not choose evil and suffering, God's aim at intensity and complexity may create discord not only between what is and what could be, but also bring forth creatures who use their freedom in ways that harm one another and the planet upon which we live.

God treasures each moment of experience, but also lures each moment toward new possibilities of experience for itself and its successors. In describing God's universal aim at higher levels of experience and interdependence, characteristic of cellular life, non-human animals, and humankind, Griffin notes that

> The process of creation can therefore be understood in terms of Jesus' message of the rule of God, according to which equal emphasis is put on the future and the present. Of course, Jesus was not thinking in terms of gradual development. But in regard to how the question of the sacred reality's activity in our world is envisioned, there is a structural parallelism: God is active in the present and for creatures to respond positively to this present activity brings immediate good; but this present activity also has an essential reference to the future, in which a greater good is intended.[41]

Still, in the process of evolution, God does not dictate but lures and persuades, even in the context of human-caused suffering and destruction. To the question, "why is there so much suffering in the world?" Griffin responds that although creaturely suffering is not necessary or pre-determined, "there could have been much less, had the creatures actualized themselves differently . . . the *possibility* of all this evil is necessary *if* there is to be the possibility of all the good that has occurred and may occur in the future."[42] God, however, never abandons our imperfect world, but seeks to transform the suffering of the world, persuasively and persistently over the long haul, into beauty of experience. More than that, God takes the pain of the world into God's own experience. God does not stand by, apathetically observing the world, but, in the words of William Blake, which can be expanded to include both masculine and feminine imagery.

He becomes a man of woe;
He doth feel the sorrow too.

Think thou canst sigh a sigh;
And thy maker is not by;
Think not thou canst wipe a tear,
And thy maker is not near.

Like the most loving parent, God feels our pain, whether it is the result of accident or intentionality, or the unintended result of God's own invitation to personal transformation and social justice. Whether the future brings healing or destruction, God is with us:

> The kingdom of God is with us today . . . [and] is the love of God for the world. It is the particular providence for particular occasions. What is done in the world is transformed into a reality in heaven, and the reality in heaven passes back into the world. By reason of this reciprocal reaction, the love in the world passes back in the love in heaven, and floods back again into the world. In this sense, God is the great companion—the fellow sufferer who understands.[43]

THE POWER OF PRAYER AND THE POWER OF GOD

As a child growing up in California's Salinas Valley in 1950s, I remember my mother placing a magnet motto on the refrigerator that announced, "Prayer changes things." As pious small town Baptists, we were praying people. We gave "thanks" at every meal, including when we ate out at restaurants. My mother blessed my brother and me when we left the house, until it became too embarrassing for us. We prayed as we began automobile trips, and we prayed in times of illness and death. On Sunday afternoons, my mother often watched the "faith healers" Oral Roberts and Kathryn Kuhlman on television as they sought to cure incurable and chronic illness through the power of prayer and healing touch.

Prayer has always been part of my life, and although I do not see prayer as a "magic bullet" or the invocation of a supernatural deity who routinely violates the laws of nature on my behalf, I pray regularly to give thanks and to join God in transforming the world and the lives of particular persons. I am deeply involved in exploring the interplay of spirituality and healing, especially in terms of healing liturgies, intercessory prayer, and the use of complementary forms of medicine in the context of Christian faith.[44]

Still, as important as prayer is in our spiritual lives, the practice of prayer raises many theological challenges and is intimately related to our vision of the interplay of divine and human power. A theology for the perplexed must relate to our daily spiritual practices as well as to global and abstract theological reflection. Over the years I have heard laypersons and pastors raise questions such as:

- Does God truly listen to our prayers?
- Does prayer change God's mind or attitude toward us?
- Does prayer enable God to do things in the world that would not have happened apart from our prayers?
- Why are some prayers answered and others unanswered?
- Can our prayers be part of a process that brings about supernatural suspensions of the laws of nature on our behalf?

While many of these questions will always remain unanswered, responsible theologians need to address with humility the everyday questions of faithful believers, for whom the practice of prayer is central to their spiritual lives. Process theology takes prayer seriously. Indeed, in a relational universe in which our thoughts and actions influence God's experiences of the world, prayer truly makes a difference for us, those for whom we pray, and for the nature of divine activity in our world and our lives. In contrast, theologies which assert that God is all-powerful, all-determining, and all-knowing in terms of past, present, and future, render our prayers of intercession and petition superfluous since our prayers cannot in any real way influence the course of already-determined events or invite support God's presence in already-known events. The practice of intercessory and petitionary prayer, prayers for the needs of others, and prayers for our own needs, require that our prayers truly make a difference to God as well as to ourselves.

Process theologians, such as Marjorie Suchocki, assert that the practice of prayer is intimately connected with our images of God's presence, activity, and relationship with the world. According to Suchocki, we need to imagine that God "is not a power over inert matter molded into form, with a single purpose, but as a power *with* all matter, present to it, pervading it with presence, with multiple purposes."[45] For Suchocki, as well as for other process theologians, a relational theology of prayer reflects God's omnipresent movements throughout the universe. Suchocki describes the intimacy of God and the world necessary to the faithful practice of prayer:

> If God's power works through presence, and if God's presence is an "omnipresence," then one could say both that there is no center to the universe and that everything in the universe is center to all else . . . we can say that all things are center, for if all things are in the presence of God, then it is God who centers them. The earth, then, is indeed privileged and we do have a privileged history, but so is every space and every history privileged, for all are presenced and centered by God. Prayer in such a universe makes eminent sense—for God is always present.[46]

From this perspective, God is, as a mystic once said, "the circle whose center is everywhere and whose circumference is nowhere."

Process theology affirms the wisdom of my mother's kitchen magnet motto, "prayer changes things." While prayer does not change God's love for us or God's quest for beauty and intensity of experience for us and all creation, our prayers open us and others to greater movements, possibilities, and energies of transformation in the God-world relationship, specifically involving those situations for whom I pray.

Marjorie Suchocki understands prayer as "our openness to the God who pervades the Universe and therefore ourselves, and therefore that prayer is also God's openness to us. In such a case, prayer is not only for our sakes but also for God's sake."[47] In a relational universe, prayer is essential to God's work in our world and "the effectiveness of God's work with the world."[48]

Prayer is intimately connected with God's vision for each moment of our lives. God's initial aim, or vision for our lives moment by moment, is grounded in God's awareness of our joys, sorrows, needs, and loves. God knows us better than we know ourselves and seeks to provide possibilities that join our lives with the lives of others in ways that bring beauty and healing to the world. God inspires us to pray for others as well as to act on their behalf. Surely this is an insightful way to interpret Romans 8:26–8:28:

> Likewise the Spirit helps us in our weakness; for we do not know how to pray as we ought, but that very Spirit intercedes with sighs too deep for words. And God, who searches the heart, knows what

is the mind of the Spirit, because the Spirit intercedes for the saints according to the will of God.

God moves within our lives, inviting us to reflect God's vision of Shalom and healing in our relationship with others, whether a child diagnosed with cancer, the survivors of the Haiti earthquake, or a friend who is in the process of discerning her or his future vocation. As Suchocki affirms, "prayer is God's invitation to us to be willing partners in the great dance that brings a world into being that reflects something of God's character."[49] Accordingly, our prayers make a difference in terms of the intensity and effectiveness of God's healing and reconciling work in the world. While the intensity and form of divine guidance and activity in the present moment of our lives is shaped—and either enhanced or limited—by our past history, decisions, values, and the quality of spiritual devotion, our attentiveness to God in the present opens us to new bursts of spiritual energy. Further, in an interdependent universe, our prayers are an example of what quantum physicists describe as non-local causation: they create a positive field of energy around those for whom we pray, enabling them to be more open to God and enabling God to be more creative and effective in shaping their life situation. In Suchocki's words,

> Since God works with the world as it is in order to bring it to what it can be, intercessory praying changes what that world is relative to the one for whom we pray, and that change is for the good. It therefore changes what God can offer that one, releasing more of the divine resources toward the good that God can then use . . . . Prayer for another's well-being allows God to weave us into the other's well-being.[50]

The question of prayer opens the issue of miracles and supernatural and unilateral acts of divine intervention to alter the events of our world. In everyday life, persons of faith pray for the cure of chronic illnesses and life-threatening cancer. We ask that God will find a way to save victims of avalanche, mine collapses, earthquakes, and tsunamis. In many cases, the answers to such prayers are beyond the resources inherent in natural processes of causation, including energetically intensified natural processes that may occur as a result of divine-human synergy. While it is clear that from time to time unexpected cures occur and persons presumed dead emerge from the rubble of falling structures, it is equally clear that these events are exceptional and that persons in similar conditions do not survive. In such situations, we must simply give thanks for their well-being without making theological judgments about the specifics of God's will or the power of certain persons' prayers. Process theology encourages people to be realistic, yet hopeful, in prayers for extraordinary life changes. Indeed, spiritual realism embraces both the concrete and the possible, regular causality and naturalistic leaps of energy. As Suchocki notes, "prayer creates as channel in the world through which God can unleash God's will toward well-being."[51] But, even when we actively seek God's movement in a particular situation, God works within that situation in all its concreteness, and not apart from the possibilities inherent in God-world call and response. For example, in the area of sickness and health, our prayers are integrated not only with God's vision and healing energy, but also issues of DNA, environment, health condition, personal attitudes, and level of health care.

As I write these words, I am daily and fervently praying for two close friends, diagnosed with life-threatening cases of cancer. I don't expect a suspension of the laws of nature to save them, but I pray for transformation that will bring them peace, pain relief, and the possibility of a cure that currently defies the medical odds for their particular diagnoses. Because each moment is unique, "miraculous" releases of energy that change our cells can occur; but there are no guarantees, except God's loving presence, in every life situation.

Process theology affirms that we can always pray for healing, or sense of God's peace, even if a cure does not occur. Further, process theologians recognize the occurrence of events described as "miracles" not as violations of the laws of nature, but of intensifications of God's healing energy as a result of the interplay of God's visionary power and energy, our prayers, and the conditions of those for whom we pray. Accordingly, process theologians can affirm that the healings of Jesus, as recorded in the gospel narratives, reflect God's choice not only to be present in Jesus in a unique way, but the interplay of Jesus' openness to God's vision and energy of Shalom and the faith of those who came in search of healing and their loved ones. These healings, process theologians believe, did not suspend the laws of nature, but were the result of greater manifestations of divine and human energy in the context of our world. Process theology affirms that we can do "greater works" (John 14:12) than we can imagine as we open to the divine energy of the universe. The natural world is more mysterious, wonderful, and energetic than we typically imagine. Extraordinary moments of transformation occur when God's vision is complemented by our prayerful openness through ritual, intercession, thanksgiving, various forms of healing touch, and the faith of a community.

How we quote scripture often reflects our theological position. Those who believe that God acts unilaterally in such a way that both ordinary and miraculous events fully reflect God's will, and that may suspend the laws of nature for certain people, tend to favor the following translation of Romans 8:28: "we know that *all things work together for good* for those who love God." They believe that God's plan triumphs over any human or non-human resistance, including terminal cancer. Process theologians favor another equally valid translation: "*in all things God works for good* for those who love God" as representative of the holistic, relational, non-coercive, and multi-factorial nature of divine activity. Surely, process theologians affirm, God is present in all things, luring them forward by God's vision of possibility for themselves and the world. But, God does not unilaterally cause all things, even good fortune, for persons of faith. In each moment, God has a dream for us and presents us with the energy to achieve it. But, God always acts relationally, receiving as well as giving, responding as well as calling. Our love of God and others, prayerfully expressed, opens the door for God to bring forth new possibilities of healing and for us to claim our role as God's partners in healing the earth. The God of process theology is the Eros of the Universe, creatively and energetically inspiring the cosmic and micro-cosmic journeys of all things, and the Holy Adventurer, preserving each moment of experience in God's everlasting life and bringing forth possibilities for the future from the world God lovingly embraces.

CHAPTER 3

TRANSFORMING CHRISTOLOGY

The second phase is the supreme moment in religious history, according to the Christian religion. The essence of Christianity is the appeal to the life of Christ as a revelation of the nature of God and his agency in the world. . . . The Mother, the Child, and the bare manger; the lowly man, homeless and self-forgetful, with his message of peace, love, and sympathy; the suffering, the agony, the tender words as life ebbed, the final despair; and the whole with the authority of supreme victory.[1]

Christology, according to process theology, is ultimately about personal and global transformation. It is not primarily an academic exercise, although Christological reflection both reveals and shapes our metaphysical and theological visions, but rather a call to creatively transform our lives, the world, and our understanding of God's presence in our personal and global experience. If Whitehead is correct in his belief that our lives are shaped in accordance with our deepest beliefs, then our beliefs about Jesus as the revelation of God's presence in the world for our healing and salvation, can be life-transforming. When Jesus asked his followers, first, "who do persons say that I am?" and, then, "who do you say that I am?" he was, in effect, asking them, "In what ways will you shape your lives around your understanding of my life and message?" When the Prologue of John's gospel (John 1:1–18) affirms that Jesus Christ reveals God's nature, it invites people to live in accordance with Jesus' pathway of healing, love, and individual and social transformation.

As a form of practical theology, Christological reflection invites us to consider our relationship to the living Christ, "How will your understanding of Jesus' life and message transform your life and your spiritual and ethical commitments?" Whitehead believed that Christianity needs to reclaim the vision of divine-human companionship, revealed in its Galilean origins.[2] The loving intimacy of Jesus' ministry reveals both God's nature and relationship with the world and inspires Jesus' followers to be God's partners in transforming the world. With Philippians 2:5–11, process theology asserts that the incarnation is best revealed in Jesus' identification with humankind and his refusal to rule the world by coercion and domination. The affirmation "every knee shall bow" defines Jesus as Christ because Jesus rules by love and not dominating power. Accordingly, his supreme victory comes through love that enables us to share his love with others in our daily lives and social involvements. Process theology affirms Jesus' non-competitive vision of spiritual leadership, revealed in the promise that when we follow Jesus' way of life, we can do "greater things" in the world in which we live. (John 14:12)

Today, in a pluralistic, postmodern era in which the future of the inhabited earth is uncertain, the question of Christology inspired John Cobb to ask, "Can Christ become good news again?"[3] In other words, will Christ's presence today in the world and in our lives contribute to healing or disease, hospitality or persecution, reconciliation or violence, and planetary care or abandonment? In this chapter, we explore the insights process theologians, such as John Cobb, David Ray Griffin, and Marjorie Suchocki for understanding: (1) the relationship between God and Jesus as the Christ, and (2) Christ's continuing impact on our lives as "savior" and "healer."

A NATURALISTIC CHRISTOLOGY

David Griffin asserts that "Jesus can only be understood as 'savior' if he is seen as the decisive clue to the nature of reality."[4] Griffin recognizes that "the problem for a Christology based on Whitehead's philosophy will be to understand not how God can be present in Jesus, but how God can be present in a special way, so that Jesus will be especially revelatory of God's nature."[5] Whereas as many Christological visions understand Jesus' uniqueness in terms of God's supernatural activity, completely different in kind from all creation, process theology asserts that "the world lives by the incarnation of God in itself."[6] God is intimately inspiring every moment of experience, through the presentation of the initial aim, or intimate and transformational vision, and the energetic lure to achieve that vision is in accordance with its own creativity. Further, process theology sees God's activity in Christ as the fullest exemplification of God's aim at creative transformation, revealed in all things and not just the Christian world. God does not operate from the outside of the universe, violating its rules and suspending its laws to achieve God's purposes; rather, God works within all things, joining order, and novelty in achieving God's vision for the universe and humankind.

Process theology affirms that "God was in Christ reconciling the world" (2 Corinthians 5:19) and that God inspired, empowered, and energized Jesus in his role as teacher, healer, and savior for people in his time and in our own. God also inspires each of us to reflect God's Christ-like vision in creative and life-supporting ways. To use the language of Martin Luther, each one of us has the potential of becoming a "little Christ," revealing God's grace by allowing divine possibilities and energy to flow through our lives to bring healing and wholeness to others. Accordingly, one clue to understand God's unique relationship to Jesus as Christ will come from process theology's understanding of God's dynamic creative-responsive love, that is, the ongoing call and response between God and each moment of Jesus' experience, in which God's choice to be more fully present in certain situations and persons, such as Jesus of Nazareth, is met by an equally transformative human response.

Process theology affirms, with the second century church father Irenaeus, that the glory of God is a human being, male or female, fully alive. With the first Christian theologians, process theology affirms that Jesus is the glory of God, joining in his life, the divine and the human response in such a way that God's vision for him became his vision for himself. Fully human, tempted and tried as we are, Jesus also reveals the nature of God and God's vision for our lives and the world. In his teachings about the reign of God, his radical hospitality toward the lost and outcast, his transformation of tradition, and his healing touch, Jesus reveals God's aim at abundant life moving through all things. As John Cobb notes, "this perfect incarnation of the Logos is at the same time the highest embodiment of humanity."[7]

Process theologians proclaim a dynamic Logos theology, echoing the affirmations of the Prologue to John's Gospel, which asserts that God's "word became flesh and lived among us" and that "the true light, which enlightens everyone, was coming into the world." (John 1:14, 9) The cosmic creativity of the Logos and Wisdom (Sophia) of

God through whom "all things came into being" (John 1:3) was the animating center of Jesus' life. Jesus was not an anomaly or alien in the universe and planetary life, but was the incarnation the Divine Logos and Wisdom, present in greater or lesser degrees in all human and planetary life. Jesus can be called the Christ, God's chosen one, because he reflects and embodies in his unique and historically-conditioned life what humans are called to become spiritually as God's beloved children, created in God's image. Accordingly, Jesus is both one of us and also something more than humankind as God's chosen revelation in our time and place.

For process theologians, the uniqueness of Christ cannot, of course, exclude God's presence in other cultures and religious traditions. If the world lives by God's incarnation, then other cultural and faith communities will experience and describe the presence of God's vision in their own unique and life-transforming ways. In the spirit of John Cobb's affirmation of Christ as the principle of creative transformation operating in all things, process theology sees Christ as the way that excludes no healing and reconciling spiritual pathway. Accordingly, process theologians, such as John Cobb, Jay McDaniel, Bruce Epperly, and Marjorie Suchocki, have been leaders in exploring the interplay of Christianity and other religious traditions.[8] Other faith traditions also reflect God's aim at healing and wholeness appropriate to their particular cultural context and ongoing understanding of human experience. Rather than alienating us from other religious traditions, Christ's message invites us to grow in "wisdom and stature" (Luke 2:52) in dialogue with the diversity of faith experiences. In the spirit of the early Logos theologians, process theology asserts that wherever truth and healing are present, God is its source whether in the Hindu ashram, the Jewish temple, the Zen meditation room, or the Islamic mosque. While the religious language and spiritual practices may differ among religious traditions, process theologians affirm that God was also present in other transformative spiritual leaders—Gautama, Mohammed, Lao Tzu, African sages, Hindu rishis, and Native American spiritual guides.

Still, process theologians must respond to the key theological question, "What makes Jesus of Nazareth unique in his revelation of God? What enables us to call him Christ, God's saving presence in our world?" A creative and insightful response is essential as process theologians enter into dialogue with creed-oriented evangelical, Orthodox, Roman Catholic, and Anglican Christians on the role of

Christ in a pluralistic, postmodern age. This response must balance the universality and intimacy of divine revelation. On the one hand, process theologians proclaim an intensely personal God who addresses all things personally in their uniqueness. Although God can be described as the creative energy of the universe, God is also the intimately personal one, the holy companion who is as intimate as our next breath. More than that, process theology asserts that God has a vision that God seeks to embody in the context of creaturely freedom and self-determination. God's aim in the universe is at beauty, complexity, and abundance, appropriate to each moment of experience and the broad expanse of planetary history. On the other hand, an ever-present and intimate God can also choose to be more present in some places than others to achieve God's vision. While each moment of experience perceives God's initial aim, or vision of possibility for it, God's aim is not passive, but the life-transforming energy inviting each moment of experience to embody the divine vision in its own unique way, given its particular history and context.

David Griffin suggests that God had a special, but not metaphysically unique, relationship with Jesus. "God's 'special' action in the world can be conceived without implying a suspension of the orderly process of causation."[9] Griffin continues, "Every event in the world is an act of God in the sense that it originates with an initial aim, derived from God. But some will be God's acts in a special sense, just as some of a man's external acts are the man's in a special sense."[10] In describing the difference between our embodiment of God's vision and Jesus' experience of God, Griffin asserts that:

> A *special act of God* would be a human act (1) in which a new vision of reality is expressed, (2) for which God's aim was a direct reflection of his eternal character and purpose, and (3) in which God's aim was actualized to a high degree. If the second and third points were actualized to an unsurpassable degree in an event in which a new vision of reality was expressed through a man's words and deeds, this would be *God's supreme act.*[11]

Marjorie Suchocki describes God's unique presence in Jesus of Nazareth as a reflection of the interplay of divine decision, human response, and cultural context.

The past and the future unite in the initial aim, leading to the creation of the present. Through these dynamics, it would be possible
for one person so to reveal both the nature of God and the nature
of what we are called to be as human beings that we could call
this person "Immanuel, God with us." Incarnation is coherent in
process thought, given the following historical conditions. First,
the past must be such that there is a readiness for this revelation.
"The fullness of time" is absolutely essential. Second, the content
of the initial aim toward incarnation must be a full communica-
tion of the nature of God. Third, the initial aim would have to
be adapted fully by the recipient . . . the finite occasion would be
"co-constituted" by the divine and human aim. Fourth, if this is
to be achieved by a human person incarnation cannot be a once-
for-all happening but it must be a continuous process.[12]

Jesus of Nazareth is unique in revealing God's wisdom and power
through the interplay of God's call and his response. Process theology asserts that the unique world view and spiritual emphasis that
Jesus Christ embodied could only have appeared in the context of the
history of the Jewish people. Jesus' life and ministry reflected the
holistic, embodied, and historical vision of the patriarchs, matri-
archs, wisdom givers, and prophets. Jesus saw himself as revealing
in a superlative way the prophetic message of Shalom. His understanding of God's movements in the world was grounded in his affirmation and creative transformation of the faith of his mothers and
fathers. Accordingly, as Clark Williamson has noted, anti-Judaism is
antithetical to the message of Jesus and his identity as God's Christ
or Messiah for our world.[13] Process theology affirms without equivocation that God continues to inspire persons within the many
streams of Judaism. Within their particular time and place, process
theologians affirm that God has inspired in world-transforming ways
other great religious figures such as Mohammed and Gautama, each
with their own unique vision of the divine and message to humankind, and will continue to do so in the future.

In more psychological language, Cobb and Griffin affirm that
"whereas Christ is incarnate in everyone, Jesus is the Christ because
the incarnation is constitutive of his very selfhood."[14] Alignment
with God's vision was the integrating center of Jesus' experiences
and encounters with the world. Cobb and Griffin assert that Jesus'

"selfhood seems to be constituted as much by the divine agency within him as his personal past."[15] Process theologians can affirm Jesus as God's Chosen One and Beloved Son without resorting to a supernatural intervention that creates an unbridgeable chasm between God's presence in Jesus and humankind.

Still, despite his personal unity with God and God's unique presence in his life, Jesus' experience—like all humans—was limited in space and time. He was a first-century Jesus male, whose understanding of the universe most likely did not include any awareness of quantum physics, contemporary Western medicine, or twenty-first century cosmology. As a fully embodied human being, Jesus' experience of God's guidance grew in response to his own intellectual and spiritual growth. Jesus was no puppet nor were his decisions eternally predetermined, but responded freely from his own selfhood to God's call to reveal and embody God's mission and love in the world. As the incarnation of God's creative love, Jesus can be called the Christ.

Scripture supports the affirmation that Jesus "grew in wisdom and stature," (Luke 2:52) that is, in his awareness of God's unique calling for him within the many dimensions of human experience. Jesus needed time for prayer and retreat as a means of maintaining his unity of spirit with God, especially when he was faced with life-changing decisions. At the Garden of Gethsemene, Jesus explored various ways to respond to the conflict that had engulfed and might even destroy him, but chose to follow God's vision even if it meant the possibility of death. When scripture recounts Jesus' affirmation, "I and the Father are one," process theologians believe that this points to an experiential and volitional unity with God, and not a metaphysical oneness that diminishes Jesus' humanity. (John 10:30) Although all things are connected with God, Jesus' connection with God was fully conscious and guided his decision-making throughout his life. Even when Jesus appears to grow in his understanding of the scope of his mission, for example, in his encounter with the Syrophonecian woman, his growth and willingness to expand his ethical and spiritual vision reflects his openness to God's inspiration: Jesus experienced new inspiration coming to him through the Syrophonecian woman's passionate and assertive love for her daughter. (Mark 7:24–30) Process theologians assert that Jesus truly experienced joy and pain, and grew in his awareness of God's vision for his life and the world.

Here, Bernard Loomer's understanding of "stature" or "size" is particularly helpful for Christological reflection. Loomer asserts that stature is the primary religious virtue and relates to the breadth of reality a person can embrace without losing his spiritual or emotional center. Jesus is the Christ because his embrace of reality in its many dimensions reflects God's own radical embrace of all things. Jesus' radical hospitality mirrors God's own commitment to seeking abundant life for all creation. Even amid the suffering and abandonment he experienced at Calvary, Jesus called out to God and chose to forgive those who were crucifying him. (Luke 23:34)

Process theology sees Jesus as the full revelation of human possibility and divine presence. His incarnation is the superlative manifestation of God's "natural" revelation among us. Here, I contend that the word "natural" embraces unheard of possibilities for personal transformation, including mystical experiences and releases of healing energy, in the context of the causal interdependence of life. In a God-inspired world, the "natural" process of causation and interdependence call us to achieve "greater things" (John 14:12) than we thought possible. If God is active as the source of energy and possibility in every moment of experience, then it is possible to affirm that there are deeper laws and powers in nature than we can imagine and may ever discover, and these laws were embodied in Jesus' first century healing ministry as well as his transformation of human lives in our time. Accordingly, the goal of process Christology is to deepen our understanding of God's presence in our everyday interactions and recognize that the natural world, rather than being one-dimensional and deterministic, contains undreamt of possibilities for healing, wholeness, and spiritual adventure.

CHRIST AS HOPE AND CREATIVE TRANSFORMATION

John Cobb asks, "Can Christ become good news again?" In the same vein, twenty-first century process theology also asks, "What positive difference does Jesus as Christ make for us in a post-modern, pluralistic context? Is Christ a living reality that still shapes our lives or a relic of the past with little or no impact on us in the present moment? If Jesus is a living reality, how does Christ change our lives?" To respond to these questions, we need to reflect on Jesus' first century mission and its impact on our lives today. Whatever we can claim for

Jesus in terms of impact and power, however, must be understood in ways that emerge from causal interdependence of life, and not supernatural interventions or predestined outcomes, such as the cross, that undermine our own or Jesus' unique creative responsiveness or the predictable order of nature.

Process theologians see Jesus as a reflection of God's aim toward creative transformation, calling humankind forward from what is to what can become. Christ calls us to be open to God now and in the future.[16] While God's aim at creative transformation is present in all things, seeking beauty, intensity, and community, God is specifically present in Jesus Christ in ways that create a life-transforming field of force among those who hear his message. The interplay of divine-human call and response resonates in all things, but Jesus Christ's life and mission creates an intensified field of force that transformed persons in the first century and still transforms persons today. Jesus Christ "saves" us, to use traditional language, by opening and empowering us to experience God's vision for our lives in new and lively ways. Jesus' life, death, and resurrection do not transform God's attitude toward us, involve Jesus paying ransom to demonic forces to liberate us, or require his suffering on our behalf in order to appease God's wrath. Rather, as the model for what we can be in our time and place, in every century, Jesus Christ calls us to become fully human as we embody in a variety of ways our vocation as God's healing partners in our world.

Process theology asserts that God's aim for the universe and human life is toward beauty and complexity of experience and, as Bernard Loomer, would assert, greater stature in our embrace and transformation of diversity, novelty, suffering, and beauty. While I will not go into Jesus Christ's mission and ministry in great detail, I believe that process theology embraces Jesus' sense of vocation, captured in the following scriptural affirmations:

The Spirit of the Lord is upon me, because he has anointed me to bring good news to the poor. He has sent me to proclaim release to the captives and recovery of sight to the blind, to let the oppressed go free, and to proclaim the year of the Lord's favor. (Luke 4:18–4:19)

Now after John was arrested, Jesus came to Galilee, proclaiming the good news of God, and saying, "The time is fulfilled, and the

kingdom of God is near; repent, and believe in the good news."
(Mark 1:14–1:15)

I came that they may have life, and have it abundantly. (John 10:10)

Living out his vocation as God's beloved messenger, fully open to
God's wisdom and power in his life, Jesus saw teaching, healing, and
transforming at the heart of his mission. Although deeply rooted in
the Jewish faith of his parents, Jesus nevertheless challenged his tradition to reflect God's all-embracing realm of Shalom, that included
oppressed and oppressor, outcast and righteous, and foreigner and
neighbor. Jesus' message and mission, process theologians assert,
was not supernaturally-oriented toward life beyond the grave, but a
call to embody God's vision for this life and this world. In this regard,
Jesus embodied the prophetic vision of Shalom, God's alternative
vision of reality in contrast to the injustices and oppression of the
world in which we live. Jesus invited persons to expect great things
of God and great things from themselves in the dynamic, life-
transforming, energetic realm of God. Jesus Christ's presence, power,
and influence in his and our own time reflect his vocation as healer,
suffering companion, and source of hope. Faithfulness to Jesus' vision
challenges us to challenge and transform our own faith tradition as
Christians in light of God's call to Shalom in our time.

Jesus Christ as Healer.[17] Fully in touch with God, Jesus was, in his
own time, an energetic field of force whose presence could transform
minds, bodies, spirits, and relationships. Jesus embodied God's aim
at shalom and healing in every area of life. Among the world's religious teachers, Jesus had a unique emphasis on whole-person, fully-
embodied healing. Among his followers, Jesus was known as a healer
who touched people's bodies, minds, and spirits, and in so doing transformed their place in the social order. The gospel narratives assert that
power (*dunamis*) flowed from Jesus that could cure physical and mental illness, whether by word, touch, forgiveness, hospitality, or ritual.
Jesus' power, congruent with today's studies on the power of prayer
and complementary medicine, could transform person's lives both
near and at a distance. To those who experienced Jesus as mediating
God's aim at wholeness in their lives, Jesus' deeds were perceived as
miraculous acts of power and energy.

While process theology does not assume a one-to-one corres-
pondence between the gospel healing stories and the actual events

recorded in the gospels, process theologians can affirm that Jesus' spiritual life and openness to God awakened in him and those he encountered to new possibilities for physical, emotional, spiritual, and relational transformation and healing. Jesus' healing power was not coercive, but reflected God's dynamic power embodied in the synergetic interplay of God's universal aim at wholeness, the faith of those he touched, and the faith of gathered friends and communities. In the spirit of quantum physics, Jesus' words, presence, and touch activated the vital, health-producing energies of the universe, reflecting God's vision of abundant life for all creation.

The healing narratives of Mark 5 are revelatory of the naturalistic, yet life-changing, character of Jesus' healing ministry. A woman who had been suffering from hemorrhages for twelve years whispers to herself, "if I touch him, I will be made well," and is transformed by an unexpected release of power that transforms her body as well as her soul. Her experience of healing reflects the synergy of human openness and divine activity. Without her faith, she would not have been healed; thus, her cure has a naturalistic component. Yet, her faith alone could not bring about the cure of her disease; she experienced a lively power flow through her. This power, however, did not come supernaturally from beyond, but from within the very flesh and blood of Jesus, that is, from his own personal, spiritual energy as it called forth her own immanent divinely-inspired healing energies. While we cannot define the nature of that power or energy, I believe that in a highly focused and magnified form, it is akin to the power released in global forms of energy medicine, such as therapeutic touch, reiki, medical Qigong, and acupuncture as well as liturgical forms of laying on of hands.[18]

In the story that accompanies the healing of the woman with the flow of blood, the healing of Jairus' daughter, Jesus evicts the naysayers and gathers a faithful group, including a young girl's parents and two disciples, as a prelude to awakening Jairus' daughter from a coma. Mark suggests in an understated way that the girl is not dead, and that her healing results from the faith of the community and Jesus' healing presence. These stories indicate that Jesus' healing was relational, rather than unilateral or coercive, in nature: he sought to join the divine quest for wholeness with individual persons' openness to divine possibilities.

Process theologians believe that God's aim at wholeness, incarnate in Jesus' healing ministry, still invites people to share in this same

healing of force through acts of prayer, healing worship, complementary medicine, social and economic transformation, and technological
medicine. In the spirit of Logos theology, the mission and ministry of
Jesus reminds us that wherever truth and healing are present, even if
Christ's name is not explicitly mentioned, God is its source. Jesus'
healings, and our own quest for healing today, are not magical or
supernatural, but draw on the divine energies of the universe residing
in ourselves and all creation.

Jesus as Suffering Companion. Alfred North Whitehead describes
God as "the fellow sufferer who understands."[19] Although process
theologians deny that the cross of Christ was foreordained or that
Jesus sacrificed his life to appease God's anger toward humankind,
nevertheless, process theology nevertheless affirms that the cross has
power to transform our lives.[20] Process theology understands the
cross in relational terms as the result of human decisions rather than
divine necessity, sacrifice, or coercion. Contrary to much "orthodox"
Christology, process theology contends that God did not want Jesus
to die, but desired that the world might believe his message of God's
reign of shalom. The crucifixion reveals the reality of our freedom to
turn away from God's vision for our lives, individually and corporately, to choose comfort rather than challenge, to succumb to group
mind rather than stand alone with integrity, and to focus on self-
interest rather than world loyalty. The African American spiritual's
words "Were you there when they crucified my Lord?" are a constant
reminder of our own ability to turn away from God in our own
moments of decision. While process theologians seldom use the word
"sin" to describe human behavior, they recognize that our failure to
embody God's highest possibilities for ourselves and the world is a
source of pain and suffering for ourselves and our neighbors.

Process theology asserts that God truly suffered with Jesus on the
cross. God envisaged a different future for Jesus than rejection and
brutality. Perhaps, God imagined what Martin Luther King described
as the "beloved community," a gently growing commonwealth beginning with Jesus' followers and growing, like the mustard seed, to
embrace the whole earth. Perhaps, even at the cross, God sought to
transform hearts and minds of those who were crucifying Jesus, but
was thwarted by people's self-interest, fear, and hatred.

Process theology suggests that God also experienced the dissonance
between the divine ideal and the stark realities of Jesus' encounter
with Pilate and the Jewish religious leaders. Like us, these religious

and political leaders could have chosen differently; they could have welcomed God's vision of Shalom embodied in Jesus' words and deeds. During Holy Week, God provided aims that were "the best for that impasse" that were disregarded by Pilate, the religious leaders, and the violent crowd. Process theology imagines that God experienced disappointment and pain at Jesus' abandonment by his disciples.

Still, God did not abandon Jesus in the Garden of Gethsemene or at Calvary. Although Jesus had moments in which he felt abandoned due to the physical pain, relational and emotional abandonment, and psychological anguish, God continued to move through his life, calling Jesus to remain at one with the divine vision for his life. Jesus' response to God's call is revealed in his forgiveness of those who were crucified with him and his care for his mother. As Marjorie Suchocki notes, "through the cross we see not only that God's love is stronger than death, but that God's love endures the pain of death, and that God's love is unconquered by death."[21]

The cross of Christ created a field of force that has endured through the centuries, calling us to personal repentance and transformation, to challenge evil in our society, and to embrace the pain of the world as God's healing companions. God's presence in Jesus' suffering calls us to action and transformation, to confront injustice, and to minimize suffering on God's behalf. The cross also comforts suffering and vulnerable persons by its witness to God's companionship and experience of their pain and grief.

Jesus Christ as Source of Hope. Jesus Christ's field of force lives on. Jesus' life, teaching, healing ministry, suffering, and resurrection create new possibilities both for God and humankind. Jesus' life in its entirety enabled God to be present in human life in new and life-transforming ways, individually and through the ambiguous, but often healing community, the church. Further, openness to Jesus' message awakens us to new possibilities for personal and community transformation.

My own life has been shaped by the message of Jesus the healer. Inspired by the healing stories of the gospels, I have come to believe that healing is possible in every situation, even when a physical cure is no longer possible. I have sought to become a healing partner of Jesus through involvement in congregational healing ministries and movements in holistic and complementary medicine. My own spiritual life has involved ongoing intercessory prayer for family, friends, and strangers, dealing with life-threatening and chronic illnesses.

Others such as Martin Luther King, Bishop Desmond Tutu, Mother Teresa of Calcutta, Dorothy Day, and Jim Wallis have seen Jesus' message of prophetic transformation as inspirational in their quest for justice. Still others see God's presence in the cross and resurrection as the source of hope as they face death or bereavement. In many ways, Jesus' followers are truly the body of Christ, Christ's hands and heart in our world today, seeking to "mend the word" (*tikkun 'olam*) in light of Jesus' revelation of God's prophetic and healing hospitality.

While process theology's vision of God as the "fellow sufferer who understands" gives new meaning to the cross, the early church's affirmation that "Christ is risen!" begs the question, "How does process theology understand resurrection as a 'natural' event, congruent with interdependent causal relationships?" Clearly, process theologians affirm that beyond the tragedy of Good Friday and the uncertainty of Holy Saturday, Easter hope bursts forth. The words of Marjorie Suchocki capture God's full involvement in the suffering and healing of the world:

> The edges of God are tragedy; the depths of God are joy, beauty, resurrection, life. Resurrection answers crucifixion; life answers death. If Jesus reveals the nature of God in his life and crucifixion, he most surely reveals God through resurrection. . . . [in the New Testament] the resurrection is the confirmation of that which Jesus revealed in his life and death, and it is the catalyst that transforms his disciples, releasing the power that led to the foundation of the church.[22]

Suchocki adds that "[t]he resurrection power of God does not annihilate the past, it transforms the past."[23] In the resurrection of Christ, we discover that "nothing can separate us from the love of God." (Romans 8:39). With Paul, we can affirm that through God's resurrection of Jesus, the ultimate tragedy of death in all its forms has been defeated. In God's memory, our lives are preserved eternally and participate in God's ongoing transformation of the world. Through God's power, we have the courage to confront evil. Through God's companionship, we are given hope amid grief and pain. While process theologians do not see resurrection as a supernatural event, violating the causal relationships of our world, I believe that process theology can affirm that Jesus was experienced by his disciples in a life-transforming, albeit mystical and mysterious, way. He was known by his wounds, the scars of suffering felt by all who are oppressed by disease and corporate injustice; but he was also recognized as one whose spirit endures despite torture and abandonment. While we cannot speculate on the mechanics of resurrection, we can affirm that God worked through this unexpected event to revive the faith and courage of the disciples and to create an energetic force that enables us to creatively confront injustice, strife, suffering, and death. Resurrection is the incarnation of God's call to abundant life, calling us to choose life for ourselves and the world, despite all that threatens personal and planetary well-being.

The post resurrection narrative of the encounter of Mary of Magdala with Jesus reflects the ongoing impact of resurrection in our lives. (John 20:11–20:18) First, the story portrays resurrection as personal as well as global. When Jesus calls her by her name, "Mary," his grieving friend is awakened to creative transformation and intimate companionship. So, in light of resurrection of Jesus, God calls us, personally and intimately, to embody his life and mission. Second, the story suggests that the risen Christ is not limited to the historical Jesus or the community that follows him. "Do not hold on to me," Jesus challenges Mary. Jesus is not bound by our images of his mission, our understanding of his resurrection, or the first century world view, but will continue to inspire people in unexpected ways, breaking down the religious walls that confine his message to the orthodox, saved, or righteous. Resurrection is a living and evolving field of force that still surprises and will continue to surprise humankind as God seeks to embrace all creation within God's healing love.

Process theologians invite us to see ourselves as part of the resurrection story. We are partners in Jesus Christ's mission today. As Cobb and Griffin note, "Christ is present to a greater or lesser extent as the creature decides for or against the Logos," God's aim at creative transformation.[24] Whether or not we fully understand God's presence in Jesus' healing, teaching, suffering, and resurrection, "acceptance of Jesus as the decisive revelation of what the divine reality is like [as creative-responsive love] opens us to being creatively transformed."[25] God continues to act in our lives through Jesus' field of force, inviting us to claim our roles as embodying Christ's continuing transformation of our world. As Cobb and Griffin affirm, "Christ can be most fully present and effective when people believe in creative transformation, understand it rightly, trust it, and open themselves to be creatively transformed."[26]

CHAPTER 4

THE SPIRIT AND THE DANCING TRINITY

It [the power of hope] is not to be found somewhere outside the organisms in which it is at work, but it is not to be identified with them either. We can conceive it best as Spirit. It is the belief in this Spirit, the giver of life and love, that is the basis of hope. In spite of all the destructive forces [we] let loose against life on this planet, the Spirit of Life is at work in ever new and unforeseeable ways, countering and circumventing the obstacles [we] put in its path. In spite of my strong tendencies to complacency and despair, I experience the Spirit in myself as calling forth the realistic hope apart from which there is no hope, and I am confident that what I find in myself is also occurring in others as well.[1]

Presence, wisdom, and power: are there grounds for extending the discussing of these attributes into an understanding of the Trinity? To follow this route is to develop a doctrine of the Trinity that is based on the human experience of God . . . . [T]he actions of God for us indicate the internal nature of God. What God is for us, God is in the depths of God's being . . . we are understanding the inner nature of God through our own experience.[2]

Process theologians have typically focused on the relationship of God and the world in terms of creative and dynamic interdependence, that is, in terms of the primordial and consequent natures of God, rather than emphasizing the doctrine of the Trinity as essential to theological reflection and spiritual experience. As John Cobb and David Griffin note, in speaking of God's nature, "the main distinction to be made is that between the creative and responsive sides of divine love"[3] rather than the three persons of the Trinity. Cobb and Griffin believe that the doctrine of the Trinity emerged initially to describe "the relation of the divine that was incarnate in Jesus to deity itself" and to assert that "it was deity itself that was incarnate in Jesus."[4] According to Cobb and Griffin, "there is only one deity which is by its nature both immanent and transcendent."[5]

Although it is essential to develop a vision of Jesus Christ's uniqueness and universality in light of the contemporary religious pluralism, the doctrine of the Holy Spirit has taken on new importance among moderate and progressive Christians as a result of the growing impact of Pentecostal and charismatic Christianity, especially in the southern hemisphere, and the growing interest in spiritual formation among progressive and mainstream Christians. In light of these emerging Christian movements, process theologians are challenged to find novel and creative ways to interpret traditional Christian doctrines, such as the Trinity, in terms of dynamic and relational, rather than static and substance-oriented categories. Further, any doctrine of the Trinity, articulated by process theologians, must affirm that the influence of each of the persons of the Trinity is universal in nature, touching the inner life of every creature as well as the ongoing evolution of the universe.

Living in the Spirit. Process theologians are clear that reality is a dynamic social process, constantly synthesizing the one and the many in the creation of each moment of experience. Although process theologians assert that the wholeness of God's vision is present in every moment of experience, God's presence in the world can be experienced in diverse and lively ways. The dancing diversity of the Trinity, reflected in the freedom of the Spirit, gives birth to a universe in which diversity reveals rather than distorts God's vision for the world. Following the insights of New Testament Christianity, process theology sees the Holy Spirit as God's immanent presence, moving within our spirits, to inspire varieties of personal and cultural gifts within the ever-evolving body of Christ.

Process theologians resonate with the Apostle Paul's descriptions of the Holy Spirit in Romans 8. Paul asserts that "When we cry 'Abba, Father!' it is that very Spirit bearing witness with our spirit that we are children of God." (Romans 8:15) Moving within the unconscious, inspiring our experience moment by moment, "that very Spirit intercedes with sighs too deep for words . . . according to the will of God." (Romans 8:26–8:27) While the Spirit moves within humankind, the Spirit also brings life and vision to all creation. Even the nonhuman world receives and responds to the inner movements of God's Spirit.

For the creation waits with eager longing for the revealing of the children of God. . . . the whole creation has been groaning in labor pains until now; and not only the creation, but we ourselves, who have the first fruits of the Sprit, groan inwardly while we wait for adoption, the redemption of our bodies. (Romans 8:19–8:23)

Our life-transforming experiences of the Holy Spirit are part of wider movement of graceful empowerment and inspiration that enlivens all things, human and nonhuman. The gifts and the graces of the Spirit are not restricted to the church, but given to all humankind and to the nonhuman world. Process theologians such as Lewis Ford describe the Spirit as the inverse of God's consequent nature, God's ongoing and expanding experience of the world: according to Ford, "the Spirit makes it possible for God to be immanent in the world (in the guise of ordinary divine aims), while the consequent nature makes it possible for the world to be immanent in God (through God's ongoing experience of the world)."[6] While the Spirit is present as the giver of life in all things, human and nonhuman, Marjorie Suchocki asserts that the spirit has a unique role in the life of the church: "the Spirit facilitates the Christian community's openness to its own transformation. The Spirit is an indwelling presence, witnessing to God through works of love."[7] Suchocki continues:

[I]f the Spirit is traditionally to be understood to be "Christ in us," an indwelling force uniting us with God and one another, whose fruits are those things that build up the community, then the Spirit might well be that element of the [initial] aim that we allow into our becoming, or the subjective aim insofar as it conforms to the Christly aim of God . . . . In other words, Christ offers creative transformation; the Spirit is creative transformation realized in the world.[8]

Norman Pittenger's understanding of the Spirit as God's indwelling presence in our lives expands on Suchocki's vision of the Spirit.

The Holy Spirit is not confined to the ecclesiastical community but is operative in the cosmos, in human history, and in every person—above all, in all response to whatever is known of God as he seeks unfailingly to disclose and give himself to his human children.[9]

Dynamic and intimate in its activity, the Spirit descends on the recently baptized Jesus, lures Jesus into the wilderness to test his vocation, and embodies Jesus' vision of transformative community in our lives today. When Jesus breathes on his disciples and says "receive the Holy Spirit" (John 20:22), his gift is a reminder that divine inspiration is present within every breath and in each moment of experience as the lure toward wholeness, transformation, and community. We live in a pan-revelational world in which God's Spirit is not an external force, but an internal reality, present in each moment's birth and throughout our life's journey. As Norman Pittenger affirms, "The Spirit of God is everywhere at work, leading men to respond to truth wherever it is found and to receive from God that which he wills to disclose in any place."[10]

The coming of the Spirit on Pentecost reflects dramatically the reality that in certain moments the Spirit present everywhere can burst forth in particular settings in new and creative ways. The universal God is also the personal Spirit, moving in the lives of individuals and communities. This Spirit is never limited by human boundaries of ethnicity, race, gender, or religion, but flows through all things, giving life and calling forth giftedness. As Peter proclaims in Acts 2:17–2:18:

I will pour out my Spirit upon all flesh, and your sons and your daughters shall prophesy, and your young men shall see visions, and your old men shall dream dreams. Even upon my slaves, both men and women, in those days I will pour out my Spirit; and they shall prophesy.

The Spirit is God's energy and inspiration within us. It inspires our personal responses to God's invitations to partnership in bringing health and vitality to every member of the body of Christ. The Spirit includes and connects everyone and all things, not just Christians or human beings. It is the breath of life that inspires us and radiates throughout the whole universe. While Paul's words in I Corinthians 12 are specifically directed toward the church as body of Christ, the same energetic inspiration that inspires the gifts of each member of Christ's ecclesiastical body also inspires Godward movements throughout the earth. When the Psalmist proclaims, "let everything that breathes praise God" (Psalm 150:6), he is affirming the dynamic call and response present in varying degrees throughout all creation.

In human life, as Karen Baker-Fletcher affirms, we are conscious of God's universal spirit as the "Spirit of truth, comfort, love, healing, and empowerment."[11] God's Spirit moves within our lives giving us courage to face injustice and seek healing for ourselves and the world.

The Spirit, accordingly, joins the inner and outer journeys of faith. God's Spirit is constantly praying within us, as Romans 8:26–8:27 asserts. The Spirit enlivens and joins our spiritual practices—prayer, contemplation, hospitality, and social concern—with what Teilhard de Chardin referred to as "the prayer of the universe" and the quest for beauty everywhere.[12] Our spiritual practices awaken us to God's Spirit and its many gifts, moving in humankind and the nonhuman world and inspiring us to acts of justice and healing for humankind and the planet. But, as the narratives of Acts of the Apostles and Romans 8 indicate, the Spirit is profoundly iconoclastic, blowing where it will as it challenges every status quo and religious legalism to embrace wider understandings of grace, revelation, and liberation.

The Spirit's movements in human life are reflected in trans-rational or mystical moments of experience. Process theology understands mysticism as a holistic phenomenon, opening new dimensions of spiritual experience and social concern. Wherever the Spirit is present, it inspires us to affirm God's intimate presence in the diversity of life in light of oneness of all creation and God's aim at healing the earth.

The Dancing Trinity. Process theologians resonate with the Eastern image of "perichoresis" as descriptive of the dancing, interdependent nature of God. God is not an unchanging substance, nor are the "persons" in the Trinity distinct and separate entities. Rather, with the Eastern Christian church, process theologians view the Trinity as lively, moving, interdependent, and intimate both within itself and within the world. In discussing the Trinity, Marjorie Suchocki and Joseph Bracken ask their fellow process theologians, "if the doctrine of the trinity is an inherently relational description of God, should not an inherently relational philosophy be helpful in expressing this doctrine?"[13] Our images of the Trinity will, accordingly, describe our world as well as God's nature. Suchocki and Bracken continue, "the model of a trinitarian God, irreducibly diverse yet one, suggests a world community of diverse events, each of which is itself richly created in and through the irreducible diversity of its members."[14]

Process theologians recognize that our vision of the Trinity has ethical and spiritual consequences. Our vision of the Trinity shapes our understanding diversity in terms of religious pluralism, race, culture, and sexual identity. Suchocki notes that the doctrine of the Trinity "implies that God, in being deepest unity, is so through infinite complexity."[15] The divine integration of unity and diversity invites us to affirm diverse forms of revelation, appropriate to each cultural context; it also challenges us to see the many faces of God revealed in the wondrous diversity of culture and sexual expression. Just as there is no privileged member of the Trinity, there is no privileged expression of life-affirming human experience.

On the whole, process theologians see an intimate connection between the *immanent* (the movements of the Trinity within Godself) and the *economic* (God's Trinitarian presence of the world) understandings of the Trinity. We encounter God as whole and united, albeit in different ways. Further, a holistic vision of the Trinity reminds us there is no "hidden" God; God's aim at beauty, complexity, and wholeness expresses God's true nature as well as God's presence in the evolving universe. There is no theological "bait and switch" in which a terrifying and wrathful God lurks behind the loving Jesus. The God, envisaged by process theologians, is awesome in grandeur, but God's majesty is defined in terms of infinite love, embracing each and every galaxy and cell. Accordingly, Marjorie Suchocki affirms "a doctrine of the trinity based on the human experience of God . . . [in which] God's actions for us include the very nature of God."[16] God is one in will and action whether God is present in human life, the history of salvation, or the evolutionary process. "What God is for us, God is in the depths of God's being."[17]

God's wholeness, however, as I implied earlier, is always reflected in a multiplicity of ways. Intimacy and diversity characterize the dynamic dance of God's inner (immanent) nature and the ever-flowing love of God's (economic) relationship with the world. Inspired by the innovative movements of the dancing Trinity, the spiritual adventure in its abundance and diversity gives birth to multiple expressions of faith and practice and challenges us to embrace and grow in our own lively dances of the spirit.

CHAPTER 5

THE HUMAN ADVENTURE

*In fact, the world beyond is so intimately entwined in our own natures
that unconsciously we identify our more vivid perspectives of it with
ourselves. For example our bodies lie beyond our own individual
existence. And yet they are a part of it. We think of ourselves as so
intimately entwined in bodily life that a man is a complex unity—
body and mind. But, the body is part of the external world, continuous
with it. In fact, it is just as much a part of nature as anything else
there—a river, mountain, or cloud. Also, if we are fussily exact, we
cannot define where a body begins and where external nature ends.[1]*

*At the heart of the nature of things, there are always the dream of
youth and harvest of tragedy. The Adventure of the Universe starts
with the dream and reaps tragic Beauty. This is the secret of the
union of Zest with Peace—That the suffering attains its end in a
Harmony of Harmonies. The immediate experiences of this Final
Fact, with its union of Youth and Tragedy, is the sense of Peace.[2]*

Process theology presents a holistic vision of human existence.
Humankind is profoundly social and embedded—body, mind, and
spirit—in the evolutionary process. As Ian Barbour asserts, "Humanity is part of nature, but a unique part. We are the product of a long
evolutionary history and retain a powerful legacy from the past. But
we also have creative abilities and potentialities without parallel
among the species of the earth."[3]

While there are many possible embodiments and goals of human
life, process theology believes that humankind is best understood in
terms of growth, adventure, interdependence, and holism. The self is
profoundly complex and relational, and intimately connected with its
physical and communal environment. Mind, body, and spirit flow

into one another in the ongoing dance of creative transformation. Spirituality is profoundly relational and embodied, and embodiment can be, conversely, a source of revelation and inspiration for spiritual transformation. In our exploration of the human adventure from a process perspective, we will consider: (1) the self as dynamic, complex, and embodied, (2) images of human wholeness and stature, (3) the reality of sin, and (4) healing and transforming grace.

THE ADVENTUROUS SELF

The human self, embracing body, mind, and spirit in dynamic interdependence, reflects the vision of reality, described by process theology. First of all, the self is a lively and ever-changing stream of experiences. In speaking of soul or mind, John Cobb asserts that the self is a "society composed of all the momentary experiences that make up the life of a person."[4] As a dynamic center of experience, the self emerges from its intimate relationship with the brain and the body, both of which constantly supply the self with novel, as well as repetitive, experiences. In contrast to images of the soul or self as an unchanging substance, unaffected by the vicissitudes of life, process theology clearly states that the "soul is not at all like a substance undergoing accidental adventures in time. It is constituted by its adventures."[5]

Process theology believes that its vision of the self as dynamic and relational reflects our everyday experience as embodied, interdependent, and constantly changing. If we reflect on our experience at this moment, we will discover that, from moment to moment, like an ever-flowing stream, our experience is in constant flux as countless thoughts, memories, unconscious influences, feelings, and sensations arise only to be replaced in the next moment by novel and emerging thoughts, memories, feelings, unconscious experiences, and sensations. Personal identity cannot be found in metaphysical stability or unchanging unity, for no absolute stability or unity can be found. Even the body, which appears to be permanent, is in constant flux; its apparent stability, necessary for personal identity, relationships, and daily life, disguises the liveliness of organs and cells that are constantly dying and being replenished. Similar to Buddhism, process theology sees the self, the center of human experience, as a stream of experiences, each of which is intimately related to the others by a common past and a projected future.[6]

Though grounded in inheritance from the past and the relative stability of the body, including the brain, the unique quality of human selfhood, Whitehead suggests, is its entertainment of unrealized possibility.[7] What is unique to humanity is that "in this genus of animals the central activity has been developed on the side of its relationship to novelty."[8] More than any other earthly creature, humankind receives and responds to God's most imaginative ideals, or initial aims, as they inspire the present and the future, and the individual and society.

Whitehead's *Adventures of Ideas* is an extended meditation on the divine aim at beauty, which has inspired and shaped the human adventure, individually and culturally, across the centuries. Process theology sees our highest humanity in terms of the quest to embody imaginative, discordant, and transformative ideals in the daily experiences of people and their communities. Could it be that the *imago dei*, or image of God in humankind, involves the dynamic, relational, and imaginative entertaining of possibilities and the quest to bring them to fruition that we share with the adventurous and possibility-seeking God? Could it be that we are most faithful to God's vision for humankind when we imaginatively envisage possibilities and then work achieve them in light of our current personal, communal, and planetary situation?

Process theology asserts that experience, value, and novelty are universal in nature, not just limited to the mind, but extending to the human body. To exist is to experience the world from a particular standpoint, whether in terms of human selfhood or cellular experience. Accordingly, process theology challenges the mind-body dualism of Descartes as well as the Newtonian vision of insentient matter, whether at the atomic, cellular, or animal levels. Mind, body, and spirit, are alive and intimately interconnected. Our thoughts and emotions shape our physical well-being as holistic and complementary medicine recognize our physical life, including our chemical balance, also shapes the quality of our emotional, mental, and spiritual life. God is present, inspiring the cells of our body toward health in the same way that God supplies the self with imaginative possibilities for personal and global transformation.

Process theology's holistic and relational understanding of the connectedness of mind, body, and spirit, provides an insightful basis for understanding the healings of Jesus, discussed in the chapter on Christology, as revealing the power of the mind and faith as factors in shaping physical well-being. Recognition of the psychosomatic unity of life is essential, accordingly, to healthy and life-affirming medicine as well as spirituality. Beyond that, process theology's recognition of mind-body-spirit intimacy provides a way of understanding the role of positive thinking and personal empowerment as factors in promoting healing from self-limiting as well as life-threatening illness.[9] Holistic spiritual formation embraces embodiment and experiences God's presence moving through the cells of our bodies as well as the inspirations of the spirit. Optimism and imagination, the grounds for hopefulness in personal and communal life, can be factors in transforming people and communities.

GROWING IN WISDOM AND STATURE

Bernard Loomer noted that one of the primary goals of religious life is the cultivation of "size" or "stature." As a model for our experiences, I have cited the affirmation of Luke 2:52 throughout this book; the recognition Jesus grew in wisdom and stature and favor with God and humankind. Jesus' stature was evident in his radical welcome of the outcasts and strangers, his willingness to face his own personal temptations, and his forgiveness of those who were crucifying him. While process theology recognizes that there are many positive expressions of human existence and, with John Cobb, affirms a variety of spiritually and culturally-based "structures of existence,"[10] process theology also sees the human adventure as part of God's holy adventure, aimed at complexity and beauty of experience. Beauty is the harmony of harmonies, bringing together contrasting experiences in a creative synthesis that is vital and complex in the present moment and in its positive impact on the future. As the work of Helene Russell suggests, the complexity of the self both reflects and opens us to the complexity and beauty of the universe.[11]

Healthy selfhood involves embracing as much of the world as possible in relationship to the values, tradition, choices, and adventures that characterize one's evolving self. Spiritual formation, accordingly, involves attentiveness to God's vision for each moment of experience; it also involves openness to God's wisdom and vision of possibility in the context of encountering other persons and their philosophical and faith traditions. The livelier the self's relationships are with the world, the more vital and beautiful the self becomes. The healthy self is imaginative and creative in its embrace of diversity.

In contrast to Rick Warren's belief that God has chosen all the important details of our lives without our input, process theology sees our personal and species future as evolving and open-ended. Adventure, freedom, and creativity are prized by God, who inspires us to create our lives and communities in partnership with God's creative wisdom.

In its quest for stature and affirmation of personal creativity, process theology sees both the body and the unconscious mind as sources of wisdom and personal growth. God speaks to us through our bodies, our health condition, and dreams and intuitions as well as the discovery of forgotten, or repressed, memories. We are healthiest when we claim the totality and multiplicity of our experience, conscious, unconscious, and relational. The self also finds wholeness through healing relationships and commitment to community and planetary well-being. Peace is a dynamic process that takes us beyond individualistic self-interest or protective denial toward "world loyalty"[12] in which our self-interest is joined with our commitment to be partners with God in the quest for beauty for all creation.[13] From this perspective, a holistic vision of the human adventure imaginatively joins body, mind, spirit, and community commitment in the fulfillment of the self and the healing of the world.

A DYNAMIC, RELATIONAL UNDERSTANDING OF SIN

God's aim at beauty, wholeness, and adventure takes many forms in many contexts. But, just as there are many ways of growing in wisdom and stature, there are also many ways to miss the mark and to fail to embody God's aim for our lives. While process theologians seldom focus on the word "sin" in their theological reflections, process theology recognizes the painful realities of brokenness, alienation, and disease. If the aim of life is to be in alignment with God's aims working through our lives and the world, then turning away from God and the dynamic interdependence of the world can be described as sinful in nature.

In the spirit of the Apostle Paul, sinful behavior can be described as missing the mark and failing to achieve the divine aim for your life as a whole or in a particular moment in your life. Turning away from God's vision of possibility limits our creativity and positive impact on others, thus impoverishing the world and our experience. Still, I must add a word of caution as it relates to our failure to embody the divine aim in our lives. From the viewpoint of process theology, all self-creation involves at least minimal deviation from God's ideal aim. God's initial aim for each moment of experience is integrated with our own response to the environment. In claiming God's initial aim as our personal subjective aim, we will necessarily inject our own creativity and freedom. Under the best of circumstances, God's vision is intended to become *our* vision; but it is important to recognize it is *our* vision, a reflection of our personal creativity, and not solely God's. This is not always a fall from grace, but may be an innovative response that adds something new to the world. Like a good parent, God does not seek absolute conformity to God's aim for us, but rather invites creatures to embody the divine vision in their own unique way. In the dynamic interplay of call and response, our creativity allows God to explore novel possibilities that would not have been relevant apart from our freedom.

However, deviating significantly from God's personal and communal vision for our lives and our relationship with others can become sinful when we consciously choose behaviors that are self-centered and harmful to ourselves and others. God's vision for each moment is never individualistic, but always has a social component. When we focus entirely on our own well-being or fixate on a particular moment of experience as definitive of our lives, we may contribute to the suffering of other creatures, both present and future. If one of the aims of life is world loyalty, then sinful behavior involves putting our individual, local, or national needs ahead of the well-being of the planet and its inhabitants.

Sin may also involve the turning away from God's aim at creative transformation by holding on to outworn traditions. In seeking to preserve a particular tradition or way of life, we may be standing in the way of the future God intends for us and our communities. We may be stifling the imaginative and innovative possibilities that are part of what it means to be created in the image of God. Process theology recognizes the importance of tradition and the preservation of the values of our faith and culture, but these are always subject to transformation in light of changing social and cultural situations. As Whitehead notes, adventure is at the heart of individual life and civilization; the pure conservative is going against the nature of the universe and the divine vision for us and our communities.[14]

Relationship is at the heart of reality, according to process theology. Accordingly, as Marjorie Suchocki notes, "relationship is the source of existence and enrichment but also sin."[15] The world from which each moment of experience arises is ambiguous in nature: along with God's vision and the goodness of creation and healthy relationships, we may also experience the impact of abusive parenting, social ostracism, racism, sexism, ageism, and heterosexism as well as garden-variety experiences of conflict and misunderstanding. These shape our experience in the moment and over a lifetime. While most process theologians speak of the original goodness of life, rather than original sin, Suchocki identifies original sin as inherited alienation, pain, and diminishment which we may repeat in our own behaviors. Sin is a social disease, inherited, although not inherent in our nature, as Augustine and Luther would maintain. Nevertheless, we often succumb to the alienation and evil we've inherited, and then pass on this woundedness and negativity in our own relationships. The impact of original sin can be seen in "any situation in which the commensurate weight of the past denies the well-being of anyone."[16] Further, according to Suchocki, sin is "participation through intent or act in unnecessary violence that contributes to the ill-being of any aspect of the earth and its inhabitants."[17] The impact of inherited alienation, narcissism, or injustice cuts off relationships and possibilities not only for individuals but for groups that have been the objects of injustice, deprivation, or scorn. Further, any injustice against creatures from oil spills and terrorist acts to corporate corruption and violence against immigrants touches the divine and diminishes God's experience of and effectiveness in our world. While process theologians do not see sin as primarily rebellion against God, the relational nature of sin touches God's existence as well as the lives of other creatures. As Suchocki notes, "sin is defined primarily from the perspective of its relation to creation, whether self or others, and only secondarily defined in relation to God."[18] Suchocki continues, "in violating the well-being of the world, we also violate the well-being of God."[19]

Finally, if God seeks persons of stature, who are able to embrace their lives and the world in its fullness, then sin may also involve, as Helene Russell notes, the inability to accept oneself in all one's multiplicity. Spirituality does not prize homogeneity but involves openness to diversity in us and others.[20] When we deny the diversity within ourselves, Russell believes, we are tempted to deny diversity in others.[21] God seeks abundant life and beauty for creation in all its diversity; failure to embrace God's aim at diversity and wholeness diminishes the complexity and vividness of our experience and the experiences of those around us. Yet, as diverse as the manifestations of sin are, God's creative gracefulness and vision of possibilities have the resources to respond to every situation of alienation and violence.

HEALING AND TRANSFORMING GRACE

Process theology maintains that in spite of the brokenness of life, we live in a grace-filled world. God is active in every moment of life, gently guiding the universe part and whole toward the possibility of greater complexity and beauty of experience. Long before the emergence of humankind, God was at work in the evolutionary process, which from the birth of this universe has reflected the interplay of creative wisdom and creaturely decision-making. The realities of beauty and conflict, and life and death, preceded the evolutionary emergence of the human species. Accordingly, process theology does not ground sin in a historically datable decision of a primordial couple. Sin as an inherited problem and chosen act emerges from a world in which the realities of cooperation and competition already existed before the emergence of humankind. Just as the experience of pain may require a certain complexity of experience, the reality of sin requires creatures who can consciously turn away from their highest personal, environmental, and communal good as well as repeat the dysfunctional and harmful behaviors of their community or family of origin.

In the midst of the ambiguity of the human condition, God's grace still abounds. Grace is not a supernatural intrusion on human experience, although it may be experienced as radically transformative of our lives and relationships. Grace is rooted in God's ever-present and tender care, revealed throughout nature, in human communities, in the depths of the unconscious as well as in insights and synchronous encounters, and, according to Christian faith, in God's movements through the Hebraic peoples and the healing presence of Jesus of Nazareth, which call us to creative transformation.

With the Apostle Paul, process theology counsels, "be not conformed to this world, but be transformed by the renewing of your mind." (Romans 12:2) Process theology recognizes that "mind," described by the Apostle Paul, is holistic in nature as the integrating center of our lives, joining embodiment, relationship, imagination, and novelty in the context of the communities in which we live. In the spirit of the Hebraic prophets, process theology sees hope for transformation emerging from healing relationships and healing communities. While the impact of inherited sin can never fully be eliminated in an interdependent world, it can be transformed through acts of reconciliation and affirmation. Although we cannot erase the results of decisions that cause pain for ourselves or others, we can open to the grace that is constantly moving in our lives, seeking in each moment "the best for that impasse."[22] In the spirit of John Wesley, process theology recognizes the transforming presence of God's grace in every situation, prior to any efforts on our part. Unlike the Calvinist tradition, God's grace is not irresistible and coercive, but persuasive and inspirational. Still, grace is constant in its intimate invitation to claim God's healing and loving care, inviting people in undramatic and dramatic ways to say "yes" to God's "yes" over and over again. No one is ultimately left behind by the persistent and graceful God.

God always calls us toward creative transformation. In our awakening to the grace of transformation, we begin a path of healing and sanctification, or spiritual transformation, in which tragedy and sin can be transformed into beauty of experience for ourselves and others. As recipients of grace, we can become Christ-like, growing in wisdom and stature, embracing our whole selves, and contributing by our healing to the healing of our communities and the planet.

CHAPTER 6

FAITH AND SCIENCE IN CREATIVE TRANSFORMATION

Religion will not regain its old power until it can face change in the same spirit as science does.[1]

Throughout this book, I have asserted that process theology is open to truth wherever it is found. Committed to its vision of dynamic interdependence and divine omnipresence, process theology asserts that Christian experience and doctrine are open-ended and constantly growing in relationship to the world. Faithfulness to Christ inspires us to embrace and promote creative transformation and explore new visions of God and human life as a result of the encounter with scientific discoveries in physics, genetics, and biology. The dynamic synergy of faith and science provides new opportunities for understanding ourselves and the universe within which we live, move, and have our being.

Process theology affirms that God is present as the inspiration of the quest for truth not only in the sanctuary but also in the laboratory. God inspires persons of faith as they worship, read the scriptures, and quietly meditate; God also inspires scientists examining fossils, exploring the genetic code, or pondering the origins of the universe. Whitehead believed that the emergence of quantum physics and the theory of evolution necessitated the reconstruction of both science and religion.[2]

Process theologians recognize that the relationship between science and religion has often been the source of controversy and intransigence on both sides. Scientists and theologians alike have denied each other's insights regarding the nature of human life and our cosmic origins. This failure of relationship has been detrimental to both faith and science. In his reflections on the relationship of science and religion, Ian Barbour notes four ways in which science and religions have approached one another.[3]

Conflict. From this perspective, faith and science are unalterably opposed to one another. If you follow one path, you must deny the other. The most well-known example of the conflict of faith and science surrounds the response of many Christians to the theory of evolution. From this perspective, whenever scripture and science conflict, Christians must hold fast to literal understandings of scripture, for example, the six day creation, the uniqueness of humankind, the original sin of Adam and Eve, the universal flood and Noah's ark, and the young earth (held to be no more than 10,000 years in age), as well as deny what they perceive to be the misguided and godless results of the theory of evolution. As one believer affirmed, "the Bible says it, I believe it, and that settles it." Even the more thoughtful approach of "intelligent design," proposed as an alternative to the theory of evolution in understanding the creation of the universe, implicitly maintains the superiority of conservative biblical scholarship and theology over the scientific method in understanding the creation of the earth and the emergence of species, and seeks to disprove any evidence that might support the theory of evolution. On the other hand, though less publicized, scientific materialism is equally adamant that religious understandings of God and human experience provide no helpful data in our understanding of the universe and human life. In fact, from the scientific materialist standpoint, the scientific method in its objectivity is the only reliable source of knowledge. From the materialist perspective, an objective study of the universe yields no evidence of purpose, spirit, or value beyond human experience. Religion can yield no helpful information about the universe or human life, and is merely an illusion, maintained to enable people to face the ultimate meaninglessness of the universe. Every phenomenon, including the human mind, can be reduced to materialistic causal relationships.

Independence. This perspective asserts that science and religion deal with parallel but unrelated realities, ask different questions, and express themselves in different languages. Science deals with objective reality, while religion deals with subjective, personal experience. Science deals with *how* things came to be, while religion asks *why* things came to be. Science deals with factual and verifiable realities, while religion deals with realities that can neither be verified nor falsified.

This dualistic approach ultimately separates reality in terms of matter and spirit, and erects an unbridgeable barrier between peoples' faith and their scientific practices.

Dialogue. Commitment to dialogue is grounded in the belief that, at their best, religion and science are open-ended, evolving, and constantly reforming in relationship to one another. Science and religion evolve in an ongoing conversation, shaping one another, despite their different approaches to understanding reality. Each provides evidence that is helpful to the other. Science depends, for example, on the religious affirmation that we live in an orderly and rational universe, worthy of scientific exploration. Conversely, the religious vision of life grows as our awareness of the cosmology, evolution, and physics evolve. The dialogue between science and religion recognizes, in light of contemporary physics, that subjectivity, freedom, and creativity are essential to the nature of things. Neither science nor religion can claim to be purely objective or fixed, but arise from our reflection on the world and its meaning for us as truth seekers, whether poring over the scriptures or meditating on photographs from the Hubble telescope.

Integration. Integration is the fruit of dialogue between religion and the sciences. Recognizing that there is only one world, faith and science seek to discern the nature of reality as they grow alongside and in relationship to one another. A truly living faith evolves, embraces, and interprets the scientific adventure, congruent with its vision of creative wisdom moving through the universe. In response to John Polkinghorne's question, "Do we have to choose between them [scientific or religious world views] or are they, instead, complementary understandings that, seen together, give us a wider picture than either on their own would provide?"[4] Process theology responds with an unequivocal "Yes!" Polkinghorne, himself a scientist-theologian, influenced by process theology, asserts that "those who seek to serve God should welcome truth from whatever corner it may come."[5] In their reflections on the theology of nature and the relationship of faith and science, Cobb and Griffin affirm that process theology enables Christians to integrate scientific truths, whether these relate to cosmology, physics, evolution, or genetics, with the Christian message of creative transformation. "We judge that Christian meaning can best be made alive today through a truly contemporary vision of the world that is at the same time truly Christian."[6] Process theologians encourage an open-ended dialogue between science and religion, whose goal is the ongoing integration of the complementary integration of these two paths, toward truth.

In the following paragraphs, I will briefly reflect on the relationship of process theology to our current understandings of cosmic and planetary evolution as one example of process theology's openness to the sciences and its commitment to constructing a flexible theological world view that contributes to both scientific and theological reflection. In the context of the current theological and cultural polarization, in which many scientists and Christians alike dismiss one another's positions or erect separate compartments for faith and science, process theology provides a way of envisaging divine activity, that embraces both the macrocosmic multi-billion year, the multi-billion galaxy cosmic adventure, from which human life emerged as well as the microcosmic world we are discovering through electron microscopes and genetic mapping.

THE PROMISE OF PURPOSE

Alfred North Whitehead spent the majority of his life as a mathematical physicist. Whitehead saw both science and religion as adventures of ideas, grounded in the quest for greater understanding of ourselves and the universe. The emergence of relativity physics, which challenged the absolute certitude claimed by Newtonian physics, shattered Whitehead's world view and convinced him that dogmatism of any kind was unwarranted. Whitehead believed that the proper approach to science, religion, and metaphysics involved openness to new and contrasting ways of looking at the universe and the human life. In contrast to scientists who denied the presence of reason or creative intelligence in the universe, Whitehead affirmed the movements of an unobtrusive counter-agency to the forces entropy operative within cosmic and planetary evolution. According to Whitehead, "animals have progressively undertaken the task of adapting the environment to themselves" in addition to being shaped by their environments.[7] This process of environmental transformation, Whitehead believed, is not wholly accidental but grounded in the pervasive, and often unconscious, aim embedded in all creation to live, live well, and to live better, reflected in the behavior of humans and non-humans alike.[8] Whereas the majority of scientists in Whitehead's era, and many scientists today, sought to deny final causation, or purpose, within the universe, Whitehead described final causation as one among many factors in the emergence of each moment of experience and implicitly in the evolutionary process itself. Further, in contrast to many scientists, Whitehead believed that the affirmation of the continuity of life, essential to the theory of evolution, required scientists, theologians, and philosophers alike to take seriously our human experience of purpose as evidence for cosmic purpose in understanding the nature of reality.

Whitehead notes that "the conduct of human affairs is entirely dominated by our recognition of foresight determining purpose, and purpose issuing in conduct."[9] Whitehead describes the following irony characteristic of certain scientific approaches to discerning the nature of reality.

Many a scientist has patiently designed experiments for the *purpose* of substantiating his belief that animal aspirations are motivated by no purposes . . . . Scientists motivated by the purpose of proving that they are purposeless constitute an interesting object of study.[10]

Whitehead even goes further to say that "the universe, as construed solely in terms of the efficient causation of purely physical connections, presents a sheer insoluble contradiction."[11] A truly open-minded approach to scientific evidence takes seriously our experience of purpose and vision. While it is reasonable, in viewing the continuity of life existing among simple and more complex organisms, to consider human behavior in terms of the stimulus-response, or, conditioning observed in the behavior of rats or mice in a maze, process theology also asks questions such as, "Isn't it just as scientific to suggest that the experiences of purpose, planning, vision, and imagination that guide human life are also present throughout the universe, albeit in more primitive forms? Couldn't we just as easily understand lower levels of experience in terms of higher levels of experience as seek to understand ourselves in terms of more primitive types of experience?"

Whitehead's image of actual occasions, integrating in their process of creation the efficient causation of the past and the internal purpose of the initial aim, directed toward the future, is his attempt to be faithful to the totality of experience, human and non-human alike. According to Whitehead, "a satisfactory cosmology must explore the interweaving of efficient and final causation."[12] In words that are foundational for any theistic understanding of the universe, Whitehead asserts that "reason is the special embodiment in us of the disciplined counteragency which saves the world."[13] In so doing, Whitehead opens the door to affirming a naturalistic theism, congruent with chance, natural selection, inheritance, and the continuity of human and non-human life, along with the possibility of the presence of mind and purpose in the evolution of the universe. Theologian John Haught goes a step further in affirming the collegial adventure of faith and science: "nothing in evolutionary theory, molecular biology, or recent physics rules out a religious interpretation of the universe as trustworthy and fulfilling."[14]

EVOLUTION AND ADVENTURE

Process theology is firmly rooted in an evolutionary understanding of the universe. Whereas some scientists deny meaning and purpose to the universe and the evolutionary process, process theology asserts that the universe as we know it, is the result of the dynamic inter-weaving of chance and purpose, and chaos and order. Conversely, while some Christians believe that God has directed the course of the universe from the very beginning, determining every detail without creaturely input, and is guiding the universe toward a pre-determined goal, process theology imagines an open-ended universe, in which God's vision is also open-ended and subject to change in relationship to creaturely decision-making and accidental occurrences.

An essential aspect of process theology, implicit throughout this text, is that the teleology of the universe is aimed at beauty and com-plexity of experience. However, there are many possible embodiments of God's vision in each moment and in the course of billions of years. Each evolutionary achievement will eventually be superseded by other embodiments of divine wisdom in the ongoing planetary and cosmic adventures. God has a vision, but not a specific and unalter-able agenda for the adventures of cosmic, planetary, and human evo-lution. Divine Creativity delights in the dance of creation, initiating steps and then responding to creation with further steps in the evolu-tion of the universe, part and whole.

According to process theology, God is constantly creating the universe. Rather than positing a clearly demarcated beginning to the universe, described theologically as creation out of nothing (*creatio ex nihilo*), process theology affirms that there has always been a creative process integrating God's vision and creaturely responsiveness. Even before the big bang, God was interacting with the primordial elements of this universe or another universe from which this universe may have emerged, as some cosmologists suggest. God has never been without a world, which provides opportunities for, and limitations of, the embodiment of God's creative vision. In contrast to those who affirm a special creation of humankind, completely separating humankind spiritually and metaphysically from other animal species, process theology asserts that humankind is embedded in the process of planetary evolution, having emerged in the course of nearly two million years' journey from *homo habilis* to today's *homo sapiens*. The fact that humans, chimpanzees, and apes share 99 percent of their DNA and have common ancestors in no way diminishes the wonder, value, and beauty of human existence.[15] In a lively meaning-filled universe of experience, to say that humans have evolved from less complex forms of life, does not deny human worth or our unique relationship with God, but places our lives in the context of a God-inspired universe in which the whole earth is full of God's glory (Isaiah 6:3) and everything that breathes praises God. (Psalm 150:6) The more we know about the course of evolution, both cosmic and planetary, the more we are filled with "radical amazement," cited as one of the primary religious virtues by Rabbi Abraham Joshua Heschel. In a lively, God-inspired universe, humans can experience something of God in every encounter and in relationship to every creature.

In contrast to conservative Christian theology, process theology asserts that God is the ultimate source of the evolutionary process. God seeks to evolve more complex and beautiful forms of experience throughout the universe. The evolutionary story is one of call and response in which God presents possibilities that inspire creaturely creativity moment by moment and over the long haul. Divine intentionality is the source of the order; and it is also the source of novelty. God does not fully determine any moment of experience, nor is God's planetary or cosmic vision embodied in a precise or predetermined way. Chance, chaos, and surprise, are built into the nature of experience, especially in more complex forms of experience. God does not seek to eliminate chance or freedom, but, like an artist or craftsperson, seeks to work within and through creaturely agency to bring about local, planetary, and cosmic environments that are able to promote complexity and beauty of experience.

As I stated earlier, process theology affirms that humankind is fully embedded in the evolutionary process. To our knowledge, we are the most complex and creative organisms on our planet. Our complexity and creativity is a call to responsible partnership in relationship with other species and the ecosphere in shaping the future evolution of our species and life on earth. In a universe of 100 billion galaxies, process theology also recognizes that the universe may contain a variety of complex life forms living in other solar systems and galaxies. Further, process theology recognizes the possibility that, given the right values and collective decisions, humankind may evolve beyond its current condition, both spiritually and physically. God is constantly luring us forward through new possibilities on the individual level as well as at the level of planetary loyalty. In contrast to Teilhard de Chardin's image of the "omega point," the Christ-consciousness toward which all things are inexorably moving, process theology recognizes many possible futures, both positive and negative, for humankind. There is no pre-determined outcome for planetary or human evolution. Our responses to God's vision of possibilities shape the planet's future, moving us closer or further away from God's open-ended vision of Shalom. Our responses as a species also shape God's presentation of possibilities within the creative process. Still, if we were to halt the evolutionary process on this planet through the use of apocalyptic weaponry or as contributors to catastrophic global climate change, God's aim at beauty will continue throughout the universe and on our planet. We humans are loved by God, who seeks creatures of stature and complexity; but God also loves the whole universe and seeks beauty in every planetary and galactic context. If humans choose the pathway of self-destruction, God will nurture other streams of evolution on earth and other planets.

The movement toward beauty and complexity is the source of higher and higher levels of experience and creativity. But, complexity of experience is ambiguous in nature and impact on the ecosphere and human relationships. David Griffin notes that there is a "positive correlation between the capacity for intrinsic goodness, on the one hand, and freedom, or the power of self-determination on the other. In the evolutionary process, the increase in the capacity of enjoying intrinsic goodness means the increase in the power to integrate harmoniously an ever-greater variety of data from the environment."[16] Still, as we discussed in Chapter 2, process theology recognizes the unavoidable reality of suffering in the course of the evolutionary process.

Higher levels of experience bring greater possibilities for both pain and beauty.

Self-determination exists in varying degrees at every level of reality, not just humankind. Accordingly, God's power must be persuasive and not coercive, whether at the amoebic or human levels of existence. To exist is to reflect as well as differentiate oneself from God's vision in the process of self-creation. The creative process has always been the result of the interplay of divine vision and creaturely response, from the moment that birthed *this* universe nearly fourteen billion years ago to the present state of human and planetary evolution.

Evolution has been a slow and often painful process and God's quest for complexity and beauty has indirectly contributed to the suffering of the world. As stated earlier, complex organisms are more sensitive to pain than simple organisms; they also can bring about greater pain for themselves and others. Greater complexity of experience is connected with greater creaturely creativity, at times tragically issuing in acts of violence and destruction as well as self-less kindness, sacrifice, and creativity that would not be possible for simpler organisms. David Griffin expresses the ambiguity of evolution by noting that "the freedom to enjoy a wide variety of bodily, moral, and religious values intensely is also the freedom to make ourselves miserable . . . precisely the same conditions that allow us to enjoy those experiences that we value most highly and would not want to live without are the conditions that lead us to suffer so intensely."[17]

As conscious agents of the evolutionary process, humans have the ability to bring greater joy or pain to one another and to their planetary companions. In the evolutionary process, "the development of high-grade actualities which can enjoy great intrinsic good necessarily means the development of effective entities which can wreak havoc."[18] Nevertheless, God persistently seeks to promote beauty and complexity amid the realities of pain and suffering, even though God cannot compel creatures or the planet as a whole to embody God's particular visions, but must work with the world as it is in terms of God's vision of what the world can become.

In contrast to those who imagine a primeval harmony, disrupted by an "original" human sin, process theologians describe the evolutionary process as the weaving of divine possibility and creaturely freedom from the very beginning. In the spirit of the Genesis creation stories, process theology affirms the essential and original goodness of creation, which includes the ability of decision-making creatures to follow, deviate, or expand in relation to God's vision. To the surprise of many more traditional theologians, process theologians recognize that deviation from God's moment by moment vision is not always bad: it may inject new possibilities into the creative process. God does not compete with, or coerce, the creative process. In fact, deviations from God's vision may enable God to be creative in new and unexpected ways. As stated earlier, while significant deviation from the highest possibilities may lead to suffering and conflict, creaturely freedom and the ability to embody God's vision in unanticipated ways is not necessarily sinful; it is simply the way things are in a universe where freedom and creativity are real. Creaturely self-determination and self-differentiation are manifestations of God's quest to balance order and novelty, tradition and creativity, and structure and freedom in the evolution of the universe. Creaturely novelty and conflict have always been part of the upward movement of the evolutionary process.

Natural selection and the conscious and unconscious quest to shape the environment in ways that promote the well-being of species are essential elements in the evolutionary process. At every level of existence, the process of evolution can be painful, especially in a universe in which experience is universal. Whitehead notes that the very process of life involves robbery and destruction of other life forms.[19] Still, God lures the universe forward to new possibilities and seeks to maximize beauty even amid conflict. Moreover, the creative-responsive God experiences both the pain and joy of creatures fully from the inside and not as an uninvolved bystander. The creator of complexity is also the recipient of the world's sorrow and celebration. Evolving people and planets takes millions and billions of years: God moves step by step eliciting beauty and complexity, overcoming entropy, and awakening and energizing possibilities.

Cosmic and planetary evolution is and will always be unfinished. Adventures in the spirit still await humankind and its cosmic companions. God is still creating in partnership with the universe. Youthful as a species, *homo sapiens* may be at the edge of new adventures of body, mind, and spirit. We have the ability to shape the earth and ourselves spiritually and technologically. The future is open and we may, by our actions, terminate the trajectory of evolution that has led from *homo habilis* to *homo sapiens* over the past two million years or we may enter into new adventures of healing the earth and explore new possibilities of human well-being and growth through

the interplay of medical, genetic, environmental, and spiritual transformation. Whether or not the human adventure continues, God
will continue to evolve the universe toward beauty and complexity.
Creation will continue in the lively and synergistic call and response
of God and the world.

CHAPTER 7

ETHICS FOR A SMALL PLANET

*Morality consists in the control of process so as to maximize
importance. It is the aim at greatness of experience in the various
dimensions belonging to it . . . . Morality is always the aim at that
union of harmony, intensity, and vividness which involves the perfection of importance for that occasion.*[1]

Process theology joins metaphysics and ethics. As Whitehead asserted
in *Religion in the Making,* a person's character is shaped by her or his
deepest beliefs about reality. Further, "[a] religion on its doctrinal
side, can thus be defined as a system of general truths which have the
effect of transforming character when they are sincerely held and
vividly apprehended."[2] Accordingly, ethics involves seeking to be in
harmony with the nature of reality as we understand it, which, from
the vantage point of process theology, reflects the presence of a
benevolent, expansive, and creative intelligence. Process ethics, as we
shall see, is profoundly theocentric and universal in its scope. While
ethical judgments often involve the relationships of humans with one
another, process ethics is grounded in a vision of the whole, which
includes the relationships of divine, human, and non-human subjects.

Process ethics seeks to overcome certain ethical dualisms that
have plagued humanity: human and non-human, individual and
society, rights and responsibilities, and duty and consequences. Each
of these polarities, or contrasts, is related to the others. For example,
process theology overcomes the dualism of deontological, or duty-
based, ethics and teleological, or consequence-based, ethics, by
asserting that God's aim for each occasion of experience is toward
intensity and beauty in the moment and in relationship to the foresee-
able future. Accordingly, our moral duty is to promote the well-being

of other creatures and insure environments that promote intensity and beauty of experience for others and for us. Our healthy self-actualization contributes to the well-being of others. The dualism of individual and society is overcome by the recognition that each moment of experience is conditioned by the environment from which it arises and then shapes, to some degree, through its process of self-creation. Individuals emerge from society, which both limits and supports their freedom of choice; but, expressions of their socially-conditioned freedom of choice must also be evaluated in terms of their impact on society and the non-human world. Ethical decision-making, accordingly, involves obligations to both our human and non-human companions. As John Cobb notes, process theology "challenges the anthropocentrism that has dominated our ethics."[3]

In its quest to overcome traditional ethical dualisms, process ethics asserts that the metaphysical principles of interdependence, experience, value, and divine inspiration shape our understanding of ethics as a discipline and our concrete ethical behavior. First of all, process theology asserts that ethical decision-making is a profoundly relational process. The interdependence of life challenges us to consider the impact of our actions on the non-human and human future, as well as on our lives and the lives of our immediate companions. As ecological thinkers have pointed out, everything is connected. Our actions radiate across the community and the world. Personal decisions are never private choices, whether they involve the termination of a pregnancy, the ending of a person's life, the closing of a factory, or a change in diet and lifestyle.

Second, ethical decision-making must take into consideration the universality of experience. Process theology maintains that all actualities have some element of experience. While experience is variable, it is clear that within the animal world, complexity of experience abounds, including the ability to experience both pain and joy. Along with the affirmation of the universality of experience comes the affirmation that non-humans have value in and of themselves, apart from their impact on human well-being. Accordingly, process theology extends the scope of ethical responsibility beyond our relationship with other humans to include the non-human world. While life, as Whitehead notes, involves consumption and, at times, destruction, we must always take into consideration the value and complexity of experience that is sacrificed for our security, pleasure, and well-being. As Whitehead asserts, "Whether we destroy or whether we preserve, our action is moral if we have safeguarded the importance of experience so far as it depends on the concrete instance of the world's history."[4] Still, process ethics invites persons to consider extending the Kantian principle of treating humans as ends (intrinsically valuable) rather than means solely for our benefit to include, at the very least, more complex species, such as dolphins, porpoises, and our relatives in the ape family. Value and complexity of experience, in whatever form it is found, deserves our respect even when we must sacrifice it for what we perceive to be a greater good.

Finally, process theology asserts that God's vision of wholeness both at the macrocosmic and microcosmic levels of reality must be taken into consideration in ethical decision-making. Jesus' words at the Sermon on the Mount can serve as guidelines for a theocentric ethic. Although we can never fully claim to know with certainty God's vision for a particular situation, we can make decisions based on our desire to embody God's will "on earth as it is in heaven." (Matthew 6:10) If, as Whitehead believes, the teleology, or aim, of the universe is toward the production of beauty—intensity, depth, and complexity of experience—then our aim in any given situation must be to contribute to individual and overall well-being in the present moment and over the long-haul. The aim at beauty and depth of experience does not preclude challenging injustice or placing limits on a child's behavior, both of which may involve conflict and discord, to achieve greater individual and corporate well-being over the long haul. An ethical system which takes beauty and wholeness as central factors must seek to maximize the conditions that allow beautiful experiences to occur, for example, quality of education, adequate income, accessibility to health care, and opportunities for cultural and moral enrichment, and the achievement of these may involve significant sacrifices and changes in the social order. Given its orientation toward the future, the prophetic quest for justice and beauty of experience is central to any process ethic.

In the context of theocentric ethics, human ethical decisions are not just about us, or even other species, they are about God's all-embracing care. As John Cobb asserts, to say that

a human life is 'of more value than many sparrows' (Matthew 10:31) does not warrant the conclusion that sparrows are worth nothing at all. Indeed, it presupposes the opposite. The Heavenly Father cares even for sparrows; how much more for human beings!

This certainly means that people too should be concerned more about a human being than a sparrow. Much more! But it does not warrant the teaching that sparrows exist only as a means to human ends . . . . God is pictured as loving the creatures and caring for them, not only human beings, but sparrows as well.[5]

What we do on earth truly matters in heaven! Whatever happens in the world contributes to the quality of God's experience. Ethical behavior, accordingly, is judged both by its congruence with God's vision for each moment of experience and its impact on God's ongoing experience of the world. Accordingly, process ethics asks questions such as, "Are our actions, individually and corporately, contributing to greater beauty in the world? Moreover, are our actions giving God a more beautiful world to experience?" Truly, in the spirit of Matthew 25, whatever we do to the "least of these," we are doing unto God, that is contributing to the quality of God's experience. Justice on earth enhances the experience of our fellow companions and also adds to God's enjoyment of the world and expands the scope of divine activity in the world. In words that join ethics and theology, Whitehead affirms that

> God's purpose in the world is quality of attainment. His purpose is always embodied in the particular ideals relevant to the actual state of the world. Thus all attainment is immortal in that it fashions the actual ideals which are God in the world as it is now. Every act leaves the world with a deeper or fainter impress of God. He then passes into his next relation with the world with enlarged, or diminished presentation of ideal values.[6]

Whitehead's comment reveals another important aspect of process ethics. Just as God's aim is contextual, ethical decisions are always contextual. As Whitehead asserts, the relational nature of life reminds us that "there is no one behavior system belonging to the essential character of the universe, as the moral ideal."[7] Process ethics joins the macrocosm and the microcosm; it also joins world consciousness with concern for each concrete moment of experience. Accordingly, as John Cobb asserts, process ethics sees rights as relational and contextual rather than absolute: "there is no basis for an *absolute* right to either life or death. All rights have to be seen in a larger perspective in which other rights are also considered. The real question is how the various rights are related to one another."[8]

Process theology maintains that ethical reflection is profoundly practical. How we view the universe shapes our behavior and, accordingly, our impact on the well-being of others and the quality of God's experience. In the following sections, I will briefly explore the resources of process theology for ethical decision-making related to (1) bioethics, (2) ecology and animal rights, and (3) economics and justice.

BIOETHICS AS PERSONAL AND RELATIONAL

Although process theologians tend to be on the liberal or progressive side of issues such as abortion and physician-assisted death, an appropriate response to matters of life and death from the standpoint of process ethics might be, "it's complicated!" In North America, Europe, and the English-speaking nations of the southern hemisphere, discussions on abortion and euthanasia are often couched in terms of absolute rights—either solely belonging to the adult decision-maker, the fetus, or God. Process theology, in contrast, sees ethical norms as relational, experiential, and contextual. Process theologians avoid absolutes in their focus on concrete ethical decisions. Further, process theology does not privilege human experience in terms of possessing absolute value. Reverence. for all life is an appropriate response to all creation at any level of experience. Being human does not set us apart from the rest of creation. Certain non-human species may, at times, experience greater complexity and rationality than human beings at certain stages of life. For example, at the time of writing this paragraph, my cat, who is currently warming himself next to my laptop, and hoping for another treat before I take my morning walk, currently has a greater complexity of experience than my grandson, who was conceived just twenty weeks ago. Both have rights and both deserve reverence; but their rights must be evaluated relationally and contextually, and in terms of potentiality. Their value does not depend on our particular human interests, but their existence as sentient beings, loved by God, with a certain complexity of experience.

Process theology, according to John Cobb, is pro-life in its affirmation that "authentic commitment [to life] should cross the boundaries separating human life from other life forms."[9] Expanding the scope of rights is not intended, Cobb asserts, "to reduce concern for human life. The purpose was to overcome the callousness this society exhibits toward the destruction of other life forms. Concern for human life should be heightened rather than diminished."[10] Cobb's argument for affirming the right to life for both humans and non-humans alike is theocentric as well as experientially-based. The very fact that creatures can experience pain places a moral claim upon us to weigh their rights along with our own needs for survival, well-being, and enjoyment. More than that, however, "God is present in all things. God's presence is the life of their lives."[11] God's eye is on the sparrow, but also on the fetus and her mother. God cares for the veal calf, but also the gourmet who enjoys veal parmesan. God moves in their lives and embraces their experiences of joy and pain as contributing to God's own experience. Still, it is obvious that some forms of suffering that we inflict on non-humans outweigh the joy we experience at the dinner table, the scent of cologne, and the convenience of petroleum products. Some costs to non-humans far outweigh the benefits to humans.[12]

From a process perspective, the ethics of abortion are profoundly relational and experiential. Both the fetus and the mother have rights to life and to pursue, consciously or unconsciously, their life projects and to actualize a whole range of possibilities inherent in human existence. While a fetus always has a right to ethical consideration, especially in terms of the future that lies ahead for him or her, process ethics recognizes that the morality of abortion is intimately related both to the fetus' current level of experience and its future possibilities and quality of life. Process theology's affirmation that God aims at beauty in all things large and small serves as an ethical foundation for affirming the appropriateness of abortion in the case of fetuses whose future lives will be brief and painful, and whose life projects will be cut short or nullified by their health conditions. Such actions are not to be taken lightly, but in the context of the best medical knowledge of the life of the unborn child. Abortion should never be a means of easy or perfunctory birth control, from the perspective of process ethics, but it must take into consideration the expected quality of experience that the child as well as her or his mother will have. There are no absolutes in this reckoning, but process theology's orientation toward maximizing intensity and beauty of experience and, consequent desire to reduce needless suffering, serves as a guideline for ethical decision-making. Further, process theology, in contrast to traditional theologies that connect life and death with God's unilateral activity, asserts that the fetus' health condition is not the result of divine decision, but many factors, ranging from diet to genetics. God does not will, in any absolute sense, the birth of every fetus; but rather seeks the highest forms of beauty and growth possible for fetus, mother, and significant others, given the anticipated outcome. From a process perspective, God does not require us to carry a radically disabled child to term, as some assert, so that the child can be an example for others or to build character or sensitivity in her or his parents.

Achieving the highest good in a particular situation or, what Whitehead describes as "the best for that impasse," may involve termination of fetal life under certain rare circumstances. A couple I know chose to end the life of their child twenty weeks after its conception, when medical tests revealed massive birth defects *in utero*. After serious conversations with their spiritual counselor and the medical team, they came to believe that God would approve their act of reducing the pain and suffering their unborn child would eventually experience in her brief lifetime. This was a painful decision for the parents, because they had already emotionally bonded with the child and had imagined their future as parents.

Despite the realities of pre-natal bonding, process theology maintains that the value and rights of the fetus are not contingent on its mother's, parents', or surrogates' love. While the love parents have toward the fetus will shape to a certain extent the future child's sense of basic trust and overall well-being, the growing fetus has a moral claim that must be taken into consideration whether or not the fetus is "wanted" by its parents or others. This right is not absolute, but it is significant. Cobb grounds the fetus' rights in potentiality rather than in their current level of experience. While a mouse may have greater complexity of experience than a fertilized ovum, the rights due to an ovum and mouse differ.

The difference is that if the human fertilized ovum is allowed to live, it will become a human being, one who should be allowed to carry out her or his projects, and hence one who has a fundamental right to life . . . . The principle favoring the right of the ovum to life is, instead, that people should support the actualization of valuable potentials, especially the potential of becoming a human being. This principle cannot be construed as absolute, but that does not make it unimportant.[13]

As the fetus grows in complexity of experience, one other factor must be considered: her or his ability to experience pain. More complex organisms, especially those with central nervous systems and complex levels of experience, are able to experience significant pain. This reality mitigates against late-term abortion except to minimize excruciating pain and disability the fetus might feel in the future or to prevent maternal death.

On the other hand, process theology affirms the preeminent rights of the mothers and other significant adults as relates to the termination of pregnancy under certain circumstances. These rights are also relational and relative. There is no absolute "right to life" for the fetus nor is abortion solely a "woman's choice." Individual rights are always conditioned by one's social and interpersonal context. To repeat Cobb's earlier comments, "all rights have to be seen in a larger perspective in which other rights are considered. The real question is how the various rights are related to one another."[14] While process theology rejects a purely individualistic understanding of rights, Cobb affirms the importance of the mother as a decision maker, whose value and future growth must be considered in carrying a fetus to term. Her own self-actualization also matters. Although process theology is humble in its connection of God's will with particular human decisions, nevertheless, there may be instances when God's vision for the highest quality of experience in terms of the relationship of the fetus and its mother includes the termination of a pregnancy. According to Cobb,

> there is justice in the current demand on the part of women that their right to decide about what happens in their bodies be respected. Because self-determination is so central to women's struggles today, this right should be given special weight . . . . Some have overstated the extent to which the fetus is part of their bodies and lacking in independent existence and value. This exaggeration is an almost necessary reaction to the continuing tendency in a patriarchal society to subordinate women's rights to those of others—the father on the one side, and the fetus on the other.[15]

Process theology affirms the importance of creativity and freedom in decision-making in the context of one's intimate relationships, health condition, and economic situation. More than that, any society that chooses to affirm the value of fetuses must equally support the value of women, their significant partners, and the importance of providing medical care, including easily accessible birth control, and economic support for every child that is born. Unlike the ethics of voluntary euthanasia, the fetus cannot consciously choose its future or decide about its survival. Accordingly, society has a bias toward insuring that every child grows up in a loving and supportive context in terms of the necessities that will enable both parent and child not only to "live, [but] to live well, and to live better."[16]

Process theologians typically recognize that physician-aided death and voluntary euthanasia are ethically acceptable actions, which may be congruent with God's vision, or initial aim, under certain circumstances. In the language of Whitehead which I have repeated throughout this text, freely chosen death may be best option for that "impasse" in the context of terminal illness, debilitating and painful chronic illness, and certain severe forms of disability. While many persons will choose to face these conditions, those for whom these conditions are burdensome beyond physical or emotional endurance are neither less moral nor less courageous than those who choose to let the illness take its course. From a theological perspective, process theology does not condemn suicide and voluntary euthanasia as unpardonable sins, or violations of God's law, contrary to God's aim at beauty, or playing God. Though neither option is desirable, sometimes death may be preferable to unremitting anguish as an expression of human and divine compassion and agency.

First, euthanasia, or physician-aided death, does not nullify God's love for us. With the Apostle Paul, process theology affirms that nothing can separate us from the love of God. (Romans 8:38–39) This includes freely chosen death as well as suicide. God does not will unendurable physical or emotional suffering, and while our decisions in this lifetime may bring us closer or take us further away from God's vision for our lives, God will continue to work in our lives seeking our wholeness in this life and the next, regardless of the circumstances of our deaths. As we will see in the chapter on survival after death, process theology asserts, contrary to traditional arguments against suicide and other forms of self-inflicted death, that a freely chosen death does not preclude God's ongoing process of healing and redemption in the afterlife.

Second, the God of process theology works concretely rather than abstractly in our lives. God's vision for us is always personal, contextual, and relational. Accordingly, while God aims at beauty in every situation, there is no *one* specific response to God's aim that is appropriate for every occasion, nor is God's vision for us unchanging in relationship to matters of life and death. A freely chosen death might be most faithful response to God's vision of possibilities in certain health situations.

Third, God's aim at beauty and complexity of experience may actually be enhanced by freely chosen euthanasia and physician-aided death. Unendurable pain and debilitation tends to narrow the scope of experience and radically diminish quality of life. In this regard, John Cobb notes that

> there is a prima facie case favoring one's right to die rather than being forced to live in a degenerating condition, should these become one's only options. First, the dread of living on casts a shadow over one's life, a darker shadow, in many cases, than the shadow cast by the expectation of death itself. This shadow could be removed only by a clear public decision that one could chose not to live in that condition.[17]

The ability to eliminate unendurable suffering may open the door to greater experience of beauty, deeper intimacy with loved ones, and openness to God's vision for one's life by freeing a terminally-ill person from the fear that he or she is condemned to die in pain. The ability to choose one's future and to eliminate future pain supports the possibility of experiencing beauty and meaning in the present moment.

Fourth, euthanasia is not, from a process perspective, "playing God." The term "playing God" assumes a theology in which God alone has the authority to decide when we die or that our lifespan has been decided in eternity without our input or consent. While we may have freedom in other parts of our lives, many traditional theologies believe that matters of life and death belong totally to God. Process theologians assert that the choice to end one's life rather than face continuing debilitation and unendurable pain is no different, in principle, than any other choice we make in the course of a lifetime.

ETHICS FOR A SMALL PLANET

If one wants to be exact, process theologians affirm that we are always "playing God" insofar as our creativity brings new things into our lives and the lives of others. While medicine, like every other human activity, can be morally ambiguous, expanding medical horizons, whether by surgical, pharmaceutical, complementary medical, or genetic means, do not go against God's will or challenge God's authority. God's aim is for us to be creative in ways that enhance life for ourselves and for our planet, and our creativity may lead to decisions that give us greater power over in shaping issues of life and death. Like a good parent, God inspires humans toward freedom and creativity, congruent with the well-being of our loved ones, communities, and the planet.

Still, the right to die through freely-chosen euthanasia or physician-aided death is not absolute, but relational and contextual. While the primary locus of choice resides in the person experiencing debilitating or life-threatening illness, the well-being of the community and loved ones also must be considered in ethical decision-making. Once again, as John Cobb notes:

> Genuinely to respect another person, as love requires, is to accept that person's right to make judgments about what he or she is to do . . . . [But] on the one hand, no one has an absolute right to act on her or his preferences, because one could be making a mistake in judgment even about one's interests, and especially because the effects on others must be considered. On the other hand, there is no basis for appealing to absolute prohibitions against taking one's life . . . . if the man is succumbing from Alzheimer's disease, the chances are that his responsibilities to others and to himself jointly support to end life with dignity and without pain before the disease has run its course.[18]

Process ethics assumes that euthanasia should always be voluntary and involve a system of public policy safeguards to encourage serious reflection as well as to protect vulnerable members of society. As always in process theology, relationship is everything—relationship with one's projected future, one's loved ones, the broader community, and God, "the fellow sufferer who understands." Process ethics recognizes that requests for physician-assisted death need to be placed in the larger context of a medical system that is truly patient-oriented in terms of the development of sophisticated palliative care as well as

113

universal accessibility to quality health care. Ethical decision-making is never an individual matter, but must be placed in the larger context of social and medical priorities. Our care for the rights of humans that begin at conception must extend through every season of human life.

ETHICS BEYOND HUMANITY

Process ethics is theocentric and global as well as personal in orientation. At the heart of process ethics is the recognition that rights are primarily relational and contextual, and not individualistic or absolute, and that ethical thinking must go beyond anthropocentrism to consider the well-being of non-humans, the survival of species, and the health of the planet as a whole. We cannot separate humankind from nature or the environment; we humans are embedded in the environment, both shaping and being shaped by the wider world beyond ourselves. Ecological, environmental, and planetary ethics are essential in our time because of our ability as humans to destroy our own species and threaten planetary life itself in unprecedented ways.

John Cobb and Charles Birch affirm that "every view of reality has ethical implications."[19] Whether dealing with physician-aided death, abortion, economic justice, genetic technology, gender equality, animal rights, and ecological issues, process ethics is guided by the basic principles of interdependence, panexperientialism, the relationship of experience and value, divine empathy, and divine inspiration. As I stated in the previous section, the experience and value of non-humans and unborn humans must be respected and taken into consideration in our ethical decision-making. As Cobb and Birch note, in commenting on the words of Jesus, "if a man is worth many sparrows then a sparrow's worth is not zero."[20] Non-humans are subjects, worthy of our respect and concern, and not insentient objects to be manipulated solely for our own benefit.

Process theologians assert that the ability to experience pain is crucial to ethical reflection. While plants can be described as democracies with no dominating center of experience, higher organisms have centered selves that enable them to experience both pleasure and pain. My two cats are not mere machines, as Rene Descartes would suggest, but rejoice in their morning breakfast, find comfort in sitting on my lap as I meditate or watch television, and enjoy playing with one another and their catnip toys. They have purposes of their own that I may choose to subordinate to my own purposes, but must take into consideration, especially if they are adamant, as cats often are, in getting what they want. They can also experience physical and emotional pain due to illness or accidents.

Value and experience extend far beyond the world of domestic animals. As Jay McDaniel states, "Christians can affirm that there is no sharp dichotomy between sentient and insentient matter and that so-called 'dead' matter is simply less sentient—less alive—than 'living' matter."[21] McDaniel recognizes that what is valuable to itself is also valuable to God, apart from human interests: "That is to say that nothing is really dead and that God's love—indeed, God's empathy—extends to mountains, rivers, stars, and wind, or at least to the momentary pulsations of unconscious and yet sentient energy of which these material forms are vast and dynamic expressions."[22]

Process theology affirms that God is in all things as a source of energy and direction *and* that all things are in God as contributors to God's ever-evolving experience of the universe. Even when the values of creatures are at cross purposes, for example, mosquitoes seeking nourishment from humans trying to enjoy a picnic, God is present luring each creature toward its appropriate expression within its environmental niche. Death is ever-present in the human and non-human worlds, but God is present throughout the evolutionary process working within the processes of cooperation as well as competition that are necessary for individual and species survival. Process theology claims that God has a vested interest in diversity, whether this diversity is individual, religious and cultural, species, or environmental. God delights in biodiversity as well as diversity in human creativity and spirituality. Accordingly, the extinction of species, mass destruction of rain forests, oil spills on the ocean, and melting of polar icecaps resulting from human actions, go against the aims of the divine artist.

God truly loves the world, part and whole. In the spirit of Proverbs 8, process theology affirms that divine creative wisdom delights in the evolving universe which is described as "good" long before humans came into being. Still, there are times in which life must be sacrificed, whether animal, vegetable, mineral, or human. Process ethics recognizes that there is no clear and absolute criterion for making judgments of value, although complexity and creativity of experience seems to be a starting point for ethical decision-making among conflicting values.

Jay McDaniel describes this dynamic and creative tension in the recognition that, on the one hand, "a life-centered ethic is rooted in respect for the intrinsic value of living beings; the value that each and every being has for itself,"[23] while, on the other hand, "intrinsic value is the experiential richness and self-concern of an organism. If some organisms have greater intrinsic value than others, it must be because their experiences are richer and their self-concern greater."[24] While challenging anthropocentric ethics, process theologians recognize that human experience, on the whole, has a greater scope of interest, embracing both past and future, and life and death, than most animal experience. This is both a source of rights and responsibilities. While we may choose to end the lives of certain animals to promote our survival and well-being, we also are responsible for justifying our destructive activities and seeking to promote species and planetary well-being. In balancing the rights of various creatures, Cobb and Birch maintain that the existence and enjoyment of non-human animals is important, "regardless of the consequences for us and for other entities. In proportion to their capacity for richness of experience we should respect them and give them consideration for making this experience possible." Our species self-affirmation, based on our survival and quality of life needs and level of experience, is always related to the value of our non-human companions: "they make a claim on us, we have duties toward them."[25]

The variability of creaturely experience does not minimize animal rights but opens the door to relational decision-making and a truly balanced ecological ethic. Cobb and Birch assert that "the recognition that every animal is an end in itself and not merely a means to human ends explodes the assumptions of our traditional ethics.[26] There are times in which we must privilege human over non-human values. Conversely, there will be times in which human values must be subordinated to the needs of individual animals and species to survive and to flourish. Beyond that, in a universe in which beauty is an essential value, grounded in divine activity and purpose, the preservation of the beauty of mountains, streams, canyons, and oceans must be considered in ethical decision-making. God aims at diverse, intricate, and dynamic planetary life, in which humans become stewards, rather than consumers and destroyers of the earth's bounty.

Jay McDaniel notes that if beauty is "the very aim of the universe and the aim of God," then "to wantonly destroy beauty in the name of progress is itself a form of sin."[27] Accordingly, McDaniel asserts that from a process perspective, ethics and spirituality are intricately connected: "The idea that God is enriched by biological diversity and harmed by violence against creation means that ethical relations with non-human forms of life cannot be separated from faithful relations to God."[28] In the spirit of the peaceable kingdom envisaged by the Hebraic prophets, humankind is called to integrate its needs with bringing health and beauty to this good earth.

A JUST AND PEACEABLE REALM

Process ethics is profoundly holistic and relational. The universe is interconnected. All that we do privately eventually radiates outward to shape relationships, the community, and the planet. Issues of economics and justice are closely connected with bioethics as well as animal rights and ecological ethics. As Herman Daly and John Cobb assert, our economic decision-making must be "for the sake of human beings and the whole biosphere."[29] Profoundly theocentric in perspective, process ethics asserts that our response to God's aim for beauty and wholeness in our lives and in the creative process beyond human experience shapes our own present experience, our personal future, and the well-being of our intimate companions and the world beyond us. Our duty is to creatively align ourselves with God's vision for the present moment for ourselves and for the communities of which we are a part.

For process theologians, God's aim at beauty resonates with the biblical quest for justice and Shalom, not just for humans but for the whole earth. Further, process theology challenges the modern world's tendency to see rights and values in terms of atomistic independence and rugged individualism rather than partnership and organic relatedness. The Apostle Paul's image of the interdependent "body of Christ," (I Corinthians 12) which balances individual and social well-being, is an apt metaphor for process social and economic ethics. Process ethical reflection challenges us to see ourselves as persons in community, whose national loyalties are balanced and shaped by world loyalty and whose self-interest is blended with concern for the community's well-being and the self-actualization of others.

The goals of justice and planetary sustainability are one and the same, according to process theologians. As John Cobb notes, "if we are persons-in-community rather than individuals-in-markets, the goal of the economy should be the expansion of communities rather than the expansion of markets."[30] In a similar fashion, Karen Baker-Fletcher asserts that "ecological justice is essential to survival, liberation, and wholeness of all our communities and of the earth. Environmental abuse cannot be separated from socioeconomic and racial discrimination."[31] In the dynamic interdependence of life, Baker-Fletcher notes, "environmental abuse, racism, sexism and classism are interlocking forms of oppression and evil . . . . When we ignore our neighbor's poisoning, we ignore our own."[32]

Process theologians recognize that our attitudes toward issues of justice, economics, and environment cannot be separated from our spiritual lives. Jay McDaniel contrasts sacramental awareness with consumerism which reduces all things to commodities.[33] The intersection of ethics and spirituality invites us to encourage an economics of appreciation in which our awareness of God's presence in all things challenges us to seek structures that enable all humans to experience beauty and wholeness in light of planetary sustainability. In the human community, the quest for justice involves providing the resources for every child and adult to experience God's dream of abundant life within the context of her or his community. The quest for justice and sustainability takes us beyond human relationships to our relationship with God and the planet as a whole. Process theology's affirmation of panentheism reminds us that "all that happens in the world enters fully into the divine life" and that "what we do to the least of our fellow creatures happens to God."[34]

God is not passive in the process of justice-seeking and healing the earth. As Monica Coleman notes, "a post-modern theology must depict a God whose vision for the world resists oppression, and describes ways in which justice can be achieved in this world."[35] God is at work in the affairs of persons and nations as the source of prophetic creativity and novel possibility. The divine restlessness challenges every institutional status quo and unjust social structure with the vision of beauty, healing, and creative transformation. Karen Baker-Fletcher adds, "God loves the earth fully. By loving one another and every sentient being—we love God. In this love we are called to resist the poisoning of peoples and the earth."[36] God is the source of alternative visions of society, which call us from self-interest to community interest and beyond community and human ethical justice to global loyalty. Whether moving in the lives of black women, the lives of non-human species, or in the quest for global economic justice and sustainability, God is, in the words of Monica Colman, making a way where there was no way "by providing possibilities that were not apparent in the experiences of the past alone."[37]

Process ethics connects means and ends in its understanding of power. Following Bernard Loomer, process theology sees the right use of power ultimately as relational and persuasive rather than unilateral and coercive, whether at the divine, human, or international levels. Justice involves the quest for common ground even in relationship with one's perceived opponents. While relational power may involve changing social structures, confronting injustice, and maintaining a just and sustainable social and planetary order, the goal of relational power is to enlarge the circle of cooperation and partnership, rather than polarize or defeat the opponent. As Mahatma Gandhi, Martin Luther King, Nelson Mandela, Dorothy Day, and Jesus affirmed, the path of peace involves inclusion and love rather than alienation and dehumanization. Certain forms of coercion may be necessary to restrain unbridled profit-seeking, enforce ecological responsibility, promote neighborhood safety, and protect individuals and the community from external threat. Still, the necessary coercive requirements of community and planetary well-being have as their goal transformation and not destruction of those who threaten our well-being. God is at work in the lives of those we challenge in our quest for justice as well as those for whom we seek justice and well-being.

Process theology recognizes that our quest for justice reflects a divine restlessness whose vision calls us to embody God's vision "on earth as it is in heaven." The quest for justice embraces the gifts of diversity whether in the biosphere or in the human community and invites us to seek wholeness for all, each creature in light of the common well-being of the whole. Through the moment by moment lure of God's initial aim, or divine inspiration toward planetary healing over the long haul, God invites us to become partners in healing the world.

CHAPTER 8

THE CHURCH IN CREATIVE TRANSFORMATION

A clash of doctrines is not a disaster—it is an opportunity . . . . Religion will not gain its old power until it can face change in the same spirit as does science. Its principles may be eternal, but the expression of these principles requires continual development. This evolution of religion is in the main a disengagement of its own proper ideas from the adventitious notions which have crept into it by reason of the expression of its own ideas in terms of the imaginative picture of the world entertained in previous ages.[1]

Many people believe that the church should be the one place that provides an unchanging message in a world of constant and unrelenting social and scientific change. To such persons, novel images of the universe, human nature, revelation, and religious diversity threaten the very survival of Christianity. They believe that clinging to traditional Christian values or literal understandings of the Biblical creation story are essential to maintaining the authority and superiority of Christianity, or their particular form of Christianity, in relation to other faith traditions. Committed to an unchanging message, they believe that faithful Christians must subordinate, if not deny, the insights of science, medicine, psychology, secular culture, and anthropology to the changeless truths of scripture and doctrine. To be faithful to Christ, the church must remain aloof from anything that challenges the "old time religion," whether it refers to the hallowed traditions of Baptists, Roman Catholics, Anglicans, Unitarians, or Pentecostals. Yet, an unchanging faith, closed off to the insights of a changing world, eventually renders ancient traditions irrelevant to the questions of seekers and the most vital ethical, spiritual, and planetary issues of the twenty first century.

In contrast to the attempt to preserve unchanging doctrinal purity, process theology recognizes that a culturally-isolated faith is a spiritual and metaphysical impossibility. In an interdependent universe, we cannot escape the impact of the social, technological, and religious environment. What we deny or dismiss in the world around us also shapes our experience and will have an impact on our faith. Process theology affirms, with Marshall McLuhan, that "the medium is the message." Traditional doctrines are profoundly changed the minute religious leaders begin using the internet, power point presentations, You Tube video clips, or social media vehicles, such as Twitter or Facebook.

Process theology surprises both traditionalists and seekers by taking an affirmative, but critical approach, to the relationship of Christianity to its cultural and scientific context. In the words of Whitehead, higher organisms, that is, living and growing organisms, originate novelty to match the novelty of their environments.[2] More than that, process theology suggests that one of the primary roles of the church is to proclaim alternative visions and inject novel possibilities that transform the world. The church as the dynamic body of Christ embraces novelty, whether spiritual, scientific, or cultural, in light of the creative wisdom of tradition and the ongoing life-changing presence of Jesus Christ. Process theology asserts that faithfulness to God requires the church to affirm and critically embrace the dynamic interdependence of life in all its varied forms. Further, faithfulness to God involves openness to God's ongoing process of creative transformation, both within and beyond the church. Process theologians embrace the Reformation insight that the reformed church is constantly reforming, and the church must be willing to transform itself to have a role in transforming the world. As Marjorie Suchocki asserts throughout her work, there is both a constant and a relative pole to proclamation that holds in tension the affirmation of God's healing and saving presence in the life, death, and resurrection of Jesus and the ongoing need for creative transformation in relationship to science, culture, and the impact of other religious traditions.

The church's openness to change is more than a matter of congregational preference or going along with social trends; it reflects the ongoing divine-human call and response present in every person's life and every community's history. Process theology asserts that God is often the primary source of discord and challenge individually, corporately, and globally. God's quest for a world that promotes beauty and complexity of experience always points to the contrast between the church as it is and the church as it is called to be in light of God's vision of beauty and Shalom. Process theologians believe that the Biblical tradition from Abraham and the prophets to Jesus and his first followers presents a vision of God as the source of novelty, adventure, and challenge to the religious and social status quo. The constancy of divine love is revealed in constantly changing forms, initiating as well as responding to the changes in our world. Accordingly, fidelity to God's vision means initiating new visions of the church and embodying them in everyday life.

Process theologians affirm that God's saving and inspiring presence is universal in scope. Wherever we find healing and truth, we will discover the presence of God, whether in the laboratory, study, soup kitchen, sanctuary, operating room, observatory, or archeological dig, even apart from explicit recognition of Christ. While the church is called to be a center of creative transformation, God's vision of transformation extends far beyond the walls of the church to embrace and inspire the spiritual and ritualistic practices of other religious traditions, new spiritual movements, and the lives of seekers, agnostics, and atheists. The church cannot claim to be the only medium of divine revelation. If divine inspiration is omnipresent, there are no God-free zones in a process world. In contrast to Cyprian's assertion that outside the church there is no salvation, process theologians proclaim that salvation—God's aim at healing and creative transformation in Jesus of Nazareth and the life of the church—can, and does, occur virtually everywhere, often dynamically outside of Christian and non-Christian institutions. Accordingly, the church's vocation is to be the living and evolving body of Christ whose ongoing task is to awaken people to God's aim at beauty, truth, and wholeness in their personal and corporate lives.

The church as a reflection of God's universal aim at creative transformation celebrates and shares God's vision of healing and Shalom for people and the planet. In the spirit of Jesus' words from the Sermon on the Mount, the church is intended to be a light in the world revealing God's presence and inviting persons to share in God's personal and planetary mission. In a God-saturated world, the church's vocation is not to be sole possessor of truth, but to invite people to experience God's vision for their lives and communities. The church, from the vantage point of process theology, is profoundly relational, embracing the wider culture, emerging technologies, multiple media and intelligences, and insights of new spiritual movements as well as traditional faiths, in light of God's vision of shalom, beauty, and justice.

A HOME FOR DIVERSITY

Process theologians proclaim that God is the ultimate source of diversity—horticultural, species, cultural, personality, ethnic, and gender. Spiritual practices and religious rituals are no exception to God's vision of diversity. There is no *one* uniform or right religious path, whether in Christianity, or the many religions of the world. God's light shines within and through African Yoruba, Asian Taoism, North American Native Religions, Celtic Christianity, Wicca and Pagan earth-based spiritualities, and Indian Hinduism and Buddhism. Each of these approaches to the divine reflects God's creative wisdom, expressed in its unique cultural context as well as in the evolving global spiritual context. Just as there is no *one* homogenous, global spirituality, there is also no *one* absolute and essential form of Christian doctrine, worship, ritual, or spirituality. Process theologians recognize that their own theological perspective is but one, albeit an insightful and inspirational, form of Christian reflection and experience. Like a prism, the light of divine creative wisdom shines through the many branches of Christianity, bringing forth different perspectives on a Truth that no *one* perspective can ever encompass. Further, because God is constantly evolving in relationship to the world, continuously integrating new possibilities with everlasting love, process theology believes that fidelity to God means willingness to be creatively transformed through commitment to our ongoing personal and communal integration of tradition and novelty. While we can never attain finality in the quest to experience or describe God's presence in the world, our openness to creative transformation deepens and expands our understanding of God's ever-evolving aim at salvation or wholeness in our world.

The church, at its best, experiences itself in terms of the diverse, yet interdependent, body of Christ. (I Corinthians 12) Paul's image of a lively interdependent body, inspired by Christ's indwelling presence, challenges congregations to become laboratories for vocation, whose task is to recognize, affirm, and bring forth the many gifts of members for their own personal well-being, the mission of the church, and the healing of the planet. Process theology takes seriously Paul's vision of unity amid diversity within the body of Christ, in which "if one member suffers, all suffer together with it; if one member is honored, all rejoice together with it." (I Corinthians 12:26) This image of Christ's body takes us even beyond the church to embrace the interconnectedness of the human community and the planetary environment.

By disposition, process theology is profoundly ecumenical. In the spirit of Bernard Loomer, process theologians see size or stature, that is, the ability of persons and institutions to embrace as much cultural and religious diversity as possible without losing their own spiritual identity, as essential to the life of the church.[3] Fidelity to Christ's presence in the church and the world challenges Christians as individuals and members of faith communities to follow the youthful Jesus in their own willingness to grow in wisdom and stature. Centered in Christ's call to transformation, hospitality, and healing, Christians can learn from one another as well as other religious traditions.

There are many "Christianities," not just one; and process theologians strain to hear the wisdom of forgotten or marginalized voices as reflecting uniquely God's presence. The quest for stature is countercultural in an era of religious culture wars. Still, while affirming their own inclusive and dynamic vision of Christianity, process theologians recognize that they can learn much from their more traditional brothers and sisters in the faith. Progressive in spirit, process theologians affirm the importance of treasuring tradition, characteristic of the Roman Catholic Church; the openness to ecstasy and healing, characteristic of Pentecostal Christians; the personal passion and love of Jesus, characteristic of evangelical Christians; the commitment to contemplative prayer, characteristic of Quakers; the emphasis on the incarnation, characteristic of Orthodox Christians; and the recognition of bedrock truths, characteristic of fundamentalist Christians. Rather than turning from dialogue, process theologians embrace dialogue with other forms of Christian worship, practice, and theology, recognizing that God is working in diverse ways in diverse denominational and theological traditions and that each tradition both opens and closes itself to the divine as a result of its particular perspective. In the growth of religion and science, "the clash of doctrines is not a disaster—it is an opportunity."[4]

Nevertheless, process theology's affirmation of Christ as the source of creative transformation may, at times, lead to challenging religious practices and doctrines that stifle God's spirit either through denying God's ongoing revelations, demanding strict and unquestioning obedience, or identifying faith with violent or destructive personal or corporate behavior. Openness to God's universal and variable presence does not mean uncritical acceptance of harmful doctrinal or behavioral practices, or positions with which we differ theologically or ethically. But, it does mean that we are always in relationship with "otherness," whether it is theological, spiritual, or cultural. As Catherine Keller asserts:

Relation does not entail relativism, which dissolves difference. Relationality implies the practice of *discernment*, which means to distinguish, to attend to difference, and to exercise good judgment. Despite the binary either/ors that back us into corners, there are always *more than two* differences.[5]

While recognizing the relativity of their own viewpoint, process theologians identify spiritual health with openness, creativity, diversity, valuing of experience, and the promotion of beauty and justice for people and the planet. Accordingly, process theology's prophetic vision humbly, yet forcefully, challenges theologies that encourage hatred, polarization, sexism, homocentrism, and violence in light of God's ongoing vision of shalom and beauty. Still, our challenge and opposition must be motivated by the quest for healing and relationship amid the diversity of theological and ethical positions. Again, Catherine Keller notes that truth emerges through dialogue with plural possibilities: "We approach not a *relativism* of anything goes— but a *relationalism* of: everything flows."[6]

Over the last hundred years, Christian experience and doctrine have evolved in relationship to religious pluralism. Open to creative transformation, process-oriented Christians can embrace the insights and spiritual practices of traditions as diverse as Hinduism, Zen Buddhism, Native American Spirituality, African Yoruba, Islamic Sufism, and North American new thought and new age movements. Process theologians believe that creative interaction with other traditions has characterized dynamic Christian faith from its origins: Paul quotes a Stoic philosopher in his message at the Athenian

Areopagus(Acts 17:28) and the author of the Gospel of John adopts Greek wisdom to speak of Jesus Christ as the Word, Logos, and Sophia of God (John 1:1–5, 9). Faithfulness to Christ means not only openness to truth wherever it is found, but integration of non-Christian spiritual practices that are congruent with the vision of the Divine love and wisdom, uniquely revealed in the life, death, teaching, and ongoing power of Christ in our lives.

A LIVING BIBLE

The bible has been described as the church's book, but in a world of global revelation, the bible is not the only book for Christian living. Contemporary Christians join biblical wisdom with the insights of psychology, Christian spiritual classics, literature, and Asian religions. Nevertheless, the scriptures play a unique and essential role in Christian formation. The bible is a book of memory, inspiration, and transformation, whose authoritative voice comes from its narrative and revelation of the divine-human call and response that inspired and challenged the Hebraic people and the first followers of Jesus, and still inspires and challenges today's Christian communities. Scripture is never the end of discussion, but the starting point for personal and social transformation. When the author of 2 Timothy 3:16 describes scripture as inspired or God-breathed, he is not calling us to embrace biblical literalism but to open ourselves to the unfettered breath of God that moves from words of scripture to the dynamic and diverse Word of Creation and Transformation moving through all things. Scripture is most alive when it is most transformational. In contrast, scripture is most deadly when its revelatory power is located in unchanging and inflexible visions of the universe, human sexuality, and divine activity. New Testament Scholar Russell Pregeant describes process theology's dynamic understanding of scripture in the following quote:

> While rejecting the notion that the Bible speaks directly and simplistically for God, they affirm its role in fostering a genuine encounter with God and a meaningful struggle to discern God's word . . . meaning emerges in the dynamic interaction of text and reader.[7]

Process theologians assert that the bible still can transform our lives when it is viewed an adventure book, calling us forward from the dualism, compartmentalization, rationalism, and one-dimensional spirituality of modernity to the holistic, relational, mystical, and energetic world that joins ancient wisdom and future possibility in the sacrament of the present moment. The bible transforms people's lives today when it is seen as an invitation for contemporary people to become part of God's ongoing holy adventure moving through their lives and communities. In a time of constant change and uncertainty, the scripture narratives of liberation, journey, healing, and justice-seeking call us to an innovative and imaginative faith.

Process theologians affirm the unique revelatory power of scripture as a book of memory, hope, and transformation, whose authority emerges from the life-changing experiences of those whose stories are narrated in scripture and in the equally life-changing experiences of those whose adventures have been inspired in their encounter with scripture. A living and intimate God does not need a literal text to transform lives, when God is already moving in our lives. Still, the scriptures witness to special moments of divine revelation and presence that created and liberated people and inspired the emergence of the first Christian communities. As a living word, the scriptures awaken us to God's presence and invite us to claim our vocation in God's quest for Shalom, for the healing of the world. Process theologians believe that the closing of the canon was not the terminus point of revelation. Revelation continues and we are part of it: like our predecessors, described in the scriptural witness, contributing our lives and words to the Spirit's revealing in our time and place. With our parents in the faith, our openness to God's transformative power in the reading of scripture enables us to share in and contribute to God's ongoing revelation in human life.

Process theologians maintain that critique of certain scriptural passages is a reflection of our fidelity to God's revelation in the scriptural tradition and in human experience. In light of a process hermeneutic, or way of interpreting scripture, grounded in the affirmation of God as the intimate and ongoing source of loving relatedness, passages that encourage genocide, sexism, heterosexism, and anti-Judaism must be challenged regardless of their status in the canonical tradition. Though relative and time bound, scripture still reflects God's quest for healing and wholeness in human life and is a source of guidance for our own spiritual adventures.

SPIRIT-CENTERED CHURCH

Process theology is profoundly theocentric in nature. God is source of energy and possibility in each moment of experience and over the course of a lifetime. God supplies the initial aim, or vision, that orients and energizes each moment of experience as it arises. While God is one of many factors that shapes our lives, moment by moment and day by day, God's vision constantly presents us with the most life-supporting and ethically-grounded possibilities, given our particular communal and cultural context. Accordingly, spirituality involves orienting our lives creatively towards God's vision for ourselves and our communities. By definition, process spirituality balances contemplation and action, personal self-actualization with social concern, and individual well-being with the health of the planet. Our spiritual experiences radiate beyond ourselves to shape our personal futures and the future of our communities. Holistic in nature, process spirituality embraces body, mind, spirit, and relationships as essential to the spiritual growth of individuals and communities. The spirit is embodied, and the body is inspired, in the interplay of divine vision and human creativity.[8]

The church, accordingly, is intended to be a laboratory for holistic spiritual formation. If God is constantly inspiring us with visions of what we can be in light of our personal experience and communal context, then the church's vocation is to awaken people to God's presence and activity in their lives and in all creation. From the standpoint of process theology, the reality of mystical experiences is undeniable. God is as near to us as our next breath, luring us forward through insights and encounters toward God's vision of beauty, truth, and goodness. Further, since God's presence is universal, then every event and encounter has the potential of becoming an epiphany, a revelation of God's vision for our lives and communities. In the quest for the divine, we don't have to travel to far off places or confine ourselves to holy sites; God is here, in, and with us. If the teleology of the universe is aimed at beauty, whether in the formation of child's life or the emergence of a galaxy, then the goal of religious institutions involves deepening our experiences of wholeness, beauty, wonder, and love, both on the individual and corporate levels.

Spirituality involves our own self-actualization as part of God's aim at bringing Shalom to our world.

Open to diverse expressions of spirituality, process theology encourages a variety of religious practices, appropriate to a person's age, personality type, life history, culture, and sociopolitical context. The intimate and lively God encourages adventurous spiritual practices, ranging from silence to chanting, yoga to centering prayer, laying on of hands to energy work. Further, process theology recognizes a variety of religious experiences. The incarnational, or embodied, nature of process theology inspires a variety of intimate encounters with God, characteristic of *kataphatic* spiritualities such as experiencing God in the natural world, the faces of the poor and one's companions, ecstatic moments of speaking in tongues, imaginative prayers or visualization practices, and word or mantra-based meditation. Yet, process theology's recognition of God's cosmic or universal presence also inspires *apophatic* or imageless spiritualities of quiet contemplation and self-emptying.

Process theology sees worship, meditation, prayer, and participation in the sacraments of the church as ways of opening to God's vision for our lives and our communities. Though present everywhere and in all persons, the divine-human call and response throughout history is heightened through our participation in life-changing rituals, such as baptism, communion, anointing with oil, laying on of hands, hospitality, and ordination. Process theology affirms the traditional definition of sacraments as visible signs of an invisible grace, emerging from divine initiative and human response over the course of centuries. The efficacy of sacraments in personal and communal transformation is both a human and divine work. As I noted in the chapter on Christology, God may choose to reveal God's vision and power more fully in certain individuals and activities, such as Jesus' breaking of bread at Passover or the baptismal practices of Judaism and the early church, both of which have become focal points of Christian spirituality. In opening to the divine presence, expressed through liturgical actions, a greater intensity of divine-human call and response occurs that can change body, mind, and spirit in the context of the natural interdependence of cause and effect.

The power of sacrament lies in part in the causal efficacy of repetition, call, and response throughout the ages. The impact of the "communion of saints" in Christian rituals, and in the rituals of other faith traditions, opens communities to new possibilities of spiritual experience today. These rituals gain power in people's lives because of the expectations and experiences of our predecessors in the faith which shape our sacramental experiences today.

Divine omnipresence and activity in human life is variable in nature and content. Accordingly, some acts and events—sacraments and theophanies—reflect God's vision more clearly than others. Still, these moments of intensity do not exclude God's saving presence in the quotidian commitments laypersons and their everyday tasks of child care, going to work, or tending for an elderly parent. Worship and the sacraments of church find their fulfillment when they remind us that all moments can be sacramental and life-changing. The universality and uniqueness of God's aim at wholeness and beauty inspire a truly lively "priesthood of all believers" in which all creatures, human and non-human, and all tasks, sacred or secular, reveal God's vision. Indeed, the goal of spiritual formation is to enable us to see that there is no distinction between sacred and secular; all moments are healing and holy, all encounters reveal divine inspiration. Our spiritual practices are intended to awaken and heighten our experience of God's ever-present visionary activity in our world.

A truly holistic spirituality inspires us to "do something beautiful for God," as Mother Teresa of Calcutta counsels.[9] In its recognition of the dynamic interplay of personal and communal aspects of existence, process theology overcomes the dualisms of body and spirit, individual and community, and spirituality and social justice. Healthy, just, and spiritually-centered communities nurture healthy people; healthy, socially-concerned, and spiritually-centered persons promote just and healthy communities.

ESCHATOLOGY AND MISSION

Lisa Withrow describes process ecclesiology as "an organic understanding of Christians gathered for the purposes of partnering with God to live in freedom and bring wholeness and love to the world."[10] In an interdependent universe, spirituality and mission are intimately connected. Our faith embraces body, mind, and spirit, and in so doing, can bring healing to ourselves and others. Beyond that, the quality and orientation of our faith, whether intended or not, radiates out into the world.

Mission is at the heart of a process-oriented church. In the intricate web of life, we cannot escape our responsibilities to our fellow

Christians and the broader human and planetary community. Faithful to God's aim at beauty and wholeness, the church is called to add beauty to the world by its message and mission. Process theology affirms the prophetic challenge of Jesus and his Hebraic spiritual parents. God calls people to seek justice, heal the sick, and protect the vulnerable. Jesus' vision of abundant life inspires the church's mission to all humankind and, insofar as possible, to the non-human world. Abundant life is intended for humankind and all creation as an essential factor in the realization of God's vision of Shalom.

The mission of the church is especially important because the personal and planetary future is both open and at risk. An open and undecided future is the source of both hope and concern. On the one hand, the world can be changed—persons can gain equality, injustices can be overturned, and the environment can be healed. This is the source of hope and empowerment in our personal and social quests for healing and justice. On the other hand, there are no guarantees, even from God, that God's vision of wholeness will be embodied in our lifetime or at all. We can severely damage or destroy the planet through our own actions—oil spills and global climate change—or seek an earth-centered spirituality and ethic.

In contrast to those whose vision of the future involves images of a "divine rescue operation" in which the faithful are rescued, while the infidel and agnostic are "left behind," process theology asserts that salvation involves world-loyalty rather than world-escape. In the global body of Christ, we are all connected; the salvation of one and the salvation of all are intimately related. More than that, process theology asserts that there is no apocalyptic, or end of the world, timetable, or predestined planetary future. The future is being shaped by our actions in the context of the ongoing dynamic divine-creaturely call and response. What we do truly matters not only in shaping our own destiny, but in contributing to the fate of the earth.

As I stated earlier, process theology promotes a holistic spirituality that sees contemplation and action as shaping and completing one another. Social transformation is intimately connected with spirituality. In describing the mission of the church in light of God's vision of the future, Marjorie Suchocki notes that "prayer changes the world."[11] Prayer not only connects us with one another and awakens us to God's creative wisdom in challenging situations, but also opens us new possibilities for creative transformation. Prayer changes who we are and what we can do; it also changes what God can do in God's ongoing quest for justice. Prayer opens the door to new bursts of possibility and energy. As Monica Coleman proclaims, our spiritual commitments "make a way where there was no way."[12]

Words inscribed on a bench at Kirkridge Retreat Center in the Pennsylvania Poconos, "picket and pray," capture the spiritually-grounded activism of process theology. In the unity of prayer and justice-seeking, process theologians recognize that God is working in the lives of oppressors as well as the oppressed. God seeks conversion of heart among oppressors and healthy and responsible self-affirmation among the oppressed. The process vision of the peaceable realm, or beloved community, emerges from the mystical recognition that God is present in all things, seeking wholeness and healing in every situation, whether personal, economic, or political.

As stated earlier, process eschatology, or the vision of the ultimate future of human and planetary life, is open-ended. Following Whitehead, process theologians do not envisage any predetermined terminus point for planetary history. God seeks beauty in our lives, in the human community, and in planetary life; but God's vision of beauty is always evolving in light of our actions and community life. For process theologians, salvation embraces the whole of life, personal and corporate, and this world and life beyond the grave. Will Beardslee asserts that: "For a process theology of hope, there is no final end, but the trust in the future which Christians express in the traditional hope for the end is taken seriously in such a theology, as is the bold Christian belief the men are called by God to participate in the fulfillment of his purpose."[13]

As the church looks toward the future, there are no guarantees that justice will roll down like waters, the swords be beaten into plowshares, the lion lie down with lamb, the church will survive, or that we can halt global climate change. But, process theologians affirm that, despite the future's uncertainty for God and ourselves, God is constantly inspiring and challenging us with new pathways of partnership in healing the world, and that even if we fail in our quest for planetary healing, our commitment and love for this planet will be treasured forevermore in the ever-evolving intimacy of divine memory.

In contrast to Tim LaHaye's vision of a world "left behind" by God, process theology asserts that God loves *this* world and has no intention of annihilating the earth and its inhabitants. God will not abandon the world in its imperfection, but constantly seeks to redeem our waywardness through God's everlasting love and inspiration of our own hopefulness. Beardslee continues: "the confidence that in spite of the waste of the world, the occasions that pass are not finally lost, but [are] recognized everlastingly in God, that gives and ultimate ground to hope in a process perspective."[14] In looking at the end of history, process theology realistically recognizes the threats of global climate change, nuclear apocalypse, and terrorism. But, process theology remains hopeful that God will continue to work in our lives and in the world, and that our hope is in God's loving and everlasting embrace of our lives and efforts to change the world. In the words of Ronald Farmer, "Rather than viewing the end as a final, static perfection, the process concept of the consequent nature of God suggests that the End should be thought of as an ongoing, serially enriched totality."[15] There is hope in history and beyond because God is the infinite and loving sense of possibilities for each moment of life and human history.

CHRISTIAN FAITH AND ANTI-JUDAISM

In the context of the ongoing transformation of the church, process theologians recognize that Christianity must come to terms with its ambiguous relationship with Judaism. Christianity embraces the wisdom of the prophets and celebrates divine revelation in the history of the Jewish people and the biblical narratives. While Jesus and his earliest followers critiqued the faith of their parents, they were deeply rooted in their Jewish heritage, which included the prophetic critique of religious practices and institutions as well as social and economic injustice. Jesus' radical hospitality, embodied in his welcome, healing, and table fellowship with outcasts and persons defined as unclean, reflected the Hebraic vision of Shalom as God's goal for history. The expansion of Christianity beyond the ethnic boundaries of Judaism also reflected the prophetic vision of God's Shalom embracing all creation.

In the aftermath of the Holocaust, or Shoah, the destruction of the Jewish people, Christian theology must embrace its Jewish roots and affirm that God's grace encompasses both the synagogue and the church.[16] Christian theology must be in conversation with Judaism, both in its practices of spiritual formation and in its reading of scripture. Process theology challenges any reading of scripture, especially an anti-Jewish reading of Jesus' arrest and crucifixion that makes

Jewish people solely responsible for Jesus' death. Just as process theologians have challenged language that promotes sexism and racism, the inclusive spirit of process theology challenges preachers, liturgists, and teachers to transform biblical texts that blatantly refer to the "Jews" to more realistic readings of scripture, such as "certain Jewish leaders" or "some Jewish people."

Process theologians affirm that the relationship of Christianity and Judaism is unique, dialogical, and mutually transformative. Today's Christians can creatively explore Jewish understandings of God's covenant with Israel and humankind, the social message of the prophets, and the spiritual resources of Jewish mysticism. Constantly open to God's renewing love, the church is called to be on a holy adventure in partnership with the God of Abraham, Isaac, Jacob, Moses, Miriam, Sarah, and Esther along with the wisdom of other religious traditions. In opening to its "older brother" Judaism as well as the wisdom of global spirituality, the church will grow in its understanding of its vocation in the twenty first century.

CHAPTER 9

SURVIVAL AFTER DEATH IN A PLURALISTIC AGE

At the heart of the nature of things, there are always the dream of youth and the harvest of tragedy. The Adventure of the Universe starts with the dream and reaps tragic Beauty. This is the secret of the union of Zest with Peace:—That the suffering attains its end in a Harmony of Harmonies. The immediate experience of this Final Fact, with its union of Youth and Tragedy, is the sense of peace. In this way the World receives its persuasion toward such perfections as are possible for its diverse individual occasions.[1]

A postmodern womanist theology understands salvation as an activity, as a kind of changing. The quest for wholeness, health, freedom, and justice involves a combination of God's activity in revealing possibilities that affirm God's vision for the world and the agency of the world . . . . Salvation is universal in that all human beings, living things, and non-living things may experience it. Still, salvation is particular and contextual for each of us, each situation, and each community in the world.[2]

Process theologians have thus far only made modest contributions to theological reflection on survival after death. When most process theologians describe everlasting life, they tend to focus on *objective immortality*, that is, our survival in God's memory and in the impact of our lives on the future. In terms of Whitehead's understanding of objective immortality, each moment of experience perishes in terms of its subjective immediacy and lives forevermore in God's ever-expanding consequent nature.

Process theologians have tended to be silent about survival after death primarily because process theology is this-worldly in orientation. Process theologians affirm that we don't have to die in order to experience God's immediate and saving presence. God is always with us in terms of the initial aim. Each moment of experience emerges from the interplay of divine possibility and creaturely influence. In many ways, even process theologians, like myself, who affirm survival after death do not describe the afterlife as a "better place," but a different environment for the ongoing adventure of divine-human call and response. Further, many process theologians see focusing on the afterlife as superfluous, and perhaps an impediment, to ethical and social justice in this lifetime. In the case of Charles Hartshorne and many other process theologians, the hope for subjective immortality is ultimately a form of self-interest. Our lives, according to Hartshorne, should be oriented toward contributing beauty to God's experience, whether or not there is survival after death. Knowing that our lives make a positive difference to the future and to God is enough! Our ethical contributions in bringing justice and beauty to the world are our immortal gifts to God, and that suffices to give our lives hope and meaning. Many process theologians rightly recognize that the promise of heaven, the threat of hell, and the understanding reincarnation in terms of progression or regression from life to life, has often served to maintain the status quo and has turned persons' attention from seeking justice in this world to waiting for a post-mortem reward. Finally, many process theologians note that most images of immortality, East and West, are couched in individualistic, rather than relational, terms. Heaven and hell, and progress and regress in the next life, are held to be the result of our individual attitudes and decisions, according to many popular visions of the afterlife, rather than the impact of culture, economics, government, and environment. Process theologians, on the whole, agree with feminist, womanist, liberation, and ecological theologians who assert that salvation is communal in nature, reflecting the significance of relationships in this life and, possibly, the next.

Many process theologians are indifferent to survival after death and, accordingly, see no need to articulate images of immortality beyond what is explicitly stated in Whitehead's philosophical system. Whitehead appears to have been agnostic in terms of our personal survival after death. What mattered to him was our everlasting survival in the divine memory. According to Whitehead:

At present it is generally held that a purely spiritual being is necessarily immortal. The doctrine here developed gives no warrant for

such belief. It is entirely neutral on the question of immortality . . . .
There is no reason why such a question should not be decided
on more special evidence, religious or otherwise, provided it is
trustworthy.[3]

In speaking of a Whiteheadian vision of life after death, John Cobb
notes that Whitehead's metaphysical system "only argues for the
possibility of life after death, not at all for its actuality. There is
nothing about the nature of the soul or the cosmos that demands
the continued existence of the living person."[4] Since we have no
definitive evidence of subjective survival after death, there is no reason to make it central to theological reflection. However, if evidence
of survival after death emerges, process theologians and philosophers
must be willing to transform their world views in light of such experiences. In recent years, the emerging body of cross-cultural research
on near death experiences, the growing interest in the afterlife among
persons who previously scorned the afterlife as an "opiate of the
masses," and the enduring importance of survival after death in the
lived experience of persons of faith challenges process theologians
to frame a vision of survival after death congruent with both the
insights of religious pluralism and the adventurous, relational, and
creative vision of reality characteristic of process theology.

Given the holistic nature of process theology, any vision of salvation
or survival after death must embrace the quest for justice in this
lifetime. While process theologians can affirm a variety of possible
images of the afterlife, to be faithful to the insights of process theology, they must affirm a clear continuity between this life and the next.
A holistic vision of salvation from a process perspective is pluralistic,
progressive, and pragmatic. In reflecting on the possibility of life after
death, process theology needs to articulate a vision of the afterlife that
affirms: (1) religious diversity and global revelation, (2) continuing
evolution beyond the grave, and (3) the relationship between the
quest for justice in this life and the quality of the afterlife. As Monica
Coleman notes, "[w]e are being saved over and over again, feeling God's
continual calling toward survival, justice, and quality of life, using each
opportunity to become in higher and more intense forms than we did
in the last occasion."[5] Survival after death must be perceived as a lively
relational process, and not a static individualistic state.

In this section, we will explore a vision of survival after death,
grounded in the insights of process theology, by considering the

following: (1) the holistic nature of salvation, (2) the scope of salvation in a pluralistic age, and (3) images of everlasting life in terms of objective and subjective immortality.

SALVATION AS HOLISTIC

Profoundly this-worldly in orientation, process theology embraces the Hebraic affirmation that "this is the day that the Lord has made; let us rejoice and be glad in it." (Psalm 118:24) This world of flesh and blood is good, and is the result of the interplay of God's creative wisdom and individual and corporate decision-making. All creation, including the non-human world, reveals God's presence; so, with the Psalmist, process theologians also proclaim, "Let everything that breathes praise God." (Psalm 150:6)

In the spirit of John's gospel, process theology asserts that eternal life is a present reality as well as a future hope. If God is omnipresent, then "heaven" and "earth" both reflect God's aim at wholeness and beauty. God is working our lives inspiring us as persons and communities to seek abundant life for all creation in the here and now, as well as in the afterlife. Though we can turn away from God's vision for our lives, God continues to lure us toward wholeness and beauty for ourselves and others. With the Logos/Sophia theology of the Prologue of John's gospel, process theologians affirm that "all things came into being through him [the Divine Word]" and "[t]he true light, which enlightens everyone, was coming into the world." (John 1:3, 9) The "Word became flesh and lived among us" both in the life and teaching of Jesus of Nazareth and in God's ongoing revelation in the universe. (John 1:14) As I stated earlier, a process vision of human life asserts that the spirit is embodied and the body is inspired. Accordingly, we can experience eternity in the ordinary events of daily life as well as ecstatic moments of self-transcendence. With Celtic Christian spirituality, process theologians affirm that all places are potentially "thin places," where divinity can be experienced in life-transforming ways.

The holistic nature of salvation indicates, first of all, that there is no dualism between this life and the next. We don't need to "go" anywhere to experience God. God is right here, present in everything we do. The quest for justice contributes to human well-being in this life as well as the next. Because there is a continuity of experience between the present life and any future experiences we may have, we are constantly creating the future by what we do today. This is at the heart of Whitehead's assertion that the initial aim, God's vision for this moment in time, is toward intensity of experience in the present moment of experience and in the immediate future. How we define the impact of the present moment on the future depends both on our vision of reality and the rootedness of our lives in our personal, planetary, and post-mortem context. If personal identity persists after physical death, then ethical responsibility reaches beyond this lifetime to include the impact of our actions on other peoples' post-mortem journeys.

If we imagine personal identity as a lively and creative stream of experiences, each moment of which emerges from a long line of predecessors, then our current experiences contribute not only to the quality of the next moment but to any future experiences we may have in this life or beyond the grave. When Mother Teresa speaks of her mission as doing something beautiful for God, she is echoing Whitehead's insight that acts of healing and kindness done in this lifetime radiate into God's experience, flood back into the world, and contribute to a positive future for ourselves and others. This positive future certainly relates to our quest for wholeness, justice, and beauty in this lifetime, but it may also pertain to any future personal experiences we may have in the afterlife.

Process theology's relational vision overcomes the critique that hope for survival after death is an impediment to social justice. Indeed, process theology affirms that our vision of the afterlife must reflect, rather than contradict, the basic principles characterizing our experience of reality in this lifetime. Our current experiences of relatedness, adventure, novelty, continuity, creativity, and openness to God's presence are carried forth into any future experiences we may have beyond the grave. With its emphasis on the universality of God's aim at wholeness and beauty, process theology asserts that alignment with God's vision requires us to seek the well-being of all creation, within the context of the basic needs of ourselves and our communities.

In line with process theology's relational vision, experiences of beauty and justice in this world shape the nature of our post-mortem experience. The quality of our post-mortem experience emerges in the dynamic interdependence of our earthly experiences as well as our specific belief systems. While faith in Christ shapes what we experience and opens us to array of divine possibilities in this lifetime and in the next, Buddhist meditation and Hindu yoga also open us to divine possibilities that will shape our afterlife. The continuity of this life and the next is not just restricted to persons of faith: if there is an afterlife, the experiences and actions of atheists and agnostics will also condition their post-mortem experience. As Jesus proclaims, God makes the "sun to rise on the evil and the good and sends rain on the righteous and unrighteous." (Matthew 5:45) In the spirit of Wesleyan tradition of theology, God's prevenient, or prior, grace embraces all creation, inspiring our growth toward fidelity and wholeness even when we are not consciously aware of it. Fundamentalists, progressives, evangelicals, moderates, agnostics, and atheists alike are subjects of divine care, inspiration, and invitation to larger visions of God and the world.

Issues such as accessibility of health care, diet, education, family of origin, and economics profoundly shape our earthly experience, both limiting and providing possibilities for our personal and corporate future. These factors also condition what God can do in our lives and what we can achieve in our own personal self-creation in this lifetime. When we seek justice in social structures, our quest involves not only ensuring that people survive, but also "live well and [to] live better."[6] Abundant life, congruent with sustaining the environment and ensuring personal well-being, is at the heart of God's quest for Shalom, reflected in our own quest for justice. Given the nature of personal identity as dynamic and relational, then the quest for justice here and now has ramifications in terms of the quality of life beyond the grave. This is surely a socially responsible understanding of the Hindu and Buddhist doctrine of karma as well as the Christian vision of resurrection and the body of Christ. We are shaping each other's experiences beyond the grave by the choices we make today and over a lifetime.

God's love never ends. Accordingly, process theology challenges traditional and dualistic understandings of afterlife in terms of heaven and hell that suggest God's attitude toward human beings changes at the moment of death. At death, these dualistic approaches assert that our lives are complete and fully decided; and then subject to divine judgment and possibility of heaven and hell. Our final breath places a limit on love and influence that even God can't overcome. Process theology takes a very different approach to divine activity in the afterlife. Given process theology's emphasis on continuity and relationship in light of God's all-encompassing and all-inspiring love, process theology contends that God continues to work within our lives at the moment of death and in whatever experiences we may have in the afterlife. God's aim at beauty and wholeness does not end at death, but continues in any possible future we might imagine or experience. Whether we live or die, we are part of God's ever-evolving and truly intimate shaping of our lives through the ongoing interplay of the concrete experience and divine possibility.

THE SCOPE OF SALVATION

Process theology affirms, without equivocation, that God is present in every moment of experience in this life and the next. As the creative energy and wisdom flowing through all things, God's presence in the world at the micro and macro levels is unambiguously aimed at beauty, wholeness, and complexity of experience. God does not possess a hidden will contrary to the divine revelation in Jesus of Nazareth and the world's other great religious teachers, nor does God eternally predestine some and not others to receive divine inspiration and motivation. While God's aim for each moment of experience is variable—"the best for that impasse"—given that moment's environment and previous choices, God's care embraces all creation and every culture. Every creature is an object of God's care. Accordingly, process theology challenges any vision of salvation that limits God's love and revelation to a particular culture or religious tradition, or separates the world and the human family into sharply divided categories of saved and unsaved or elect and reprobate.

The scope of salvation and revelation are both universal and personal from the perspective of process theology. In fact, the universal and personal are complementary aspects of God's dynamic and intimate presence in each moment of experience and throughout history. What is unique about process theology's understanding of the interplay of salvation and revelation is its affirmation that our ongoing experiences of revelation and, accordingly, salvation are variable in intensity and content. There is no absolute form or norm of revelation. God has many names and ways to address people and cultures. As I discussed in the chapter on Christology, God can choose to be more active in some persons and places than others as a result of the dynamic interplay of call and response, and revelation and reception, in the lives of persons and communities. Further, the content of revelation differs in accordance to our cultural setting, personal history, and previous decisions. As Marjorie Suchocki notes, "God is involved incarnationally in every culture, and therefore God's leading is also reflected in each culture's conceptual schemes. This leads to multiple forms of truth as conceptualizations of various communal experiences."[7] Accordingly, "God not only calls religions into existence, but is present in all religions . . . . God is radically incarnate, whether explicitly in Christianity, or implicitly in other religions."[8]

The truth that Christians experience in the life and teachings of Jesus is global and not parochial. What we describe as Christ or Logos, the embodiment of God's creative transformation in Jesus of Nazareth, takes on different nuances in different cultural settings, and may be understood in a variety of ways, depending on culture and context. As Jay McDaniel asserts, "the good news, therefore, is that the Spirit of Christ is not reducible to Christianity, Christ is more than Christianity."[9] In articulating a theology of world religions, process theology supports "the view that the insights of the many religions are different but complementary, such that no religion contains all the truth even as all contain some of the truth."[10]

Yet, the scope of revelation and salvation cannot be restricted merely to persons participating in the great religious traditions of the world. God speaks to and through all creation, inviting agnostics, seekers, and even atheists to experience wholeness, beauty, and creative transformation. Long before the emergence of the great world religions, God was moving through the indigenous religions of Africa, Australia, and the Americas. While distortion and denial of God's vision can occur both within and outside communities of faith, God still addresses each person in ways that are appropriate to her or his personal situation, belief system, and ethical decisions. Conversely, our openness to diverse and insightful spiritual truths within our own as well as other religious traditions enables God to be more active in the presentation of spiritual and ethical possibilities to persons and communities.

In the holistic and relational universe affirmed by process theology, the traditional distinctions of saved and unsaved or special and general revelation cannot be sustained. God seeks the salvation of all humankind, and though humans may choose to disregard God's moment by moment invitations, God continues to act in our lives in this lifetime and in any possible post-mortem existence. Further, while some revelatory experiences are congruent with God's vision in such a way that they enlighten the whole of human experience, for example, the lives and teachings of Jesus and Gautama, these revelatory experiences are not different in kind from the everyday experiences of the divine available to all people. All revelation is to some degree "special" insofar as it is addressed concretely to individuals in particular cultural and relational contexts. God has a personal relationship with each and every creature, regardless of its level of experience or environmental context.

Truth is manifold, according to process theologians. Using the metaphor of a kaleidoscope, God's revelations vary according to the movements of our lives. While the recognition of certain aspects of divine are more pronounced in particular cultural contexts, all faith communities identify aspects of the divine from the vantage point of their particular cultural and spiritual history. As Christians, we experience the divine through the lens of the life and teaching of Jesus of Nazareth. Yet, even Christian experience is variable, pluralistic, and evolving. For example, some Christians experience Christ through personal encounters in which Jesus truly meets me in the garden and "walks with me and talks with me and tells me I am his own."[11] Others encounter Jesus in the quest for social justice and environmental sustainability. Still others experience the holy in mystical experiences of unity with God. Pluralism is a reality not only among the world religions, but within each religious tradition. Though Gautama, Mohammed, and Jesus still inspire and shape the experiences of their followers, there is no static essence of any religious tradition. In fact, in some cases, there is a greater experiential affinity among persons across religions than within a particular religious tradition, for example, Jewish and Christian contemplatives or social activists may have more in common with one another than they do with text-oriented literalists. As we discussed in the chapter on the church, process theology sees Christianity as constantly evolving and branching out in new forms in the context of the interplay of tradition, the current situation, and God's future vision which holds the past and present in creative tension.

In conclusion, process theology sees revelation and salvation as an ongoing process, joining intimacy and universality. God's aim is to save all creation, and God provides transformational possibilities in each moment of experience and over a lifetime of experiences. God intimately reveals divine possibilities in all creation in accordance with each person's and community's context. As humans, living in communities of faith, we constantly shape the nature of revelation, experiencing God's presence from our perspective and the perspective of our faith communities. Accordingly, a person's or community's experience of revelation may expand and evolve or contract and die as a result of the quality of its openness to the wisdom of the world's great religions and spiritual practices. In today's pluralistic age, our images of salvation and the afterlife, accordingly, must evolve in the context of growing interfaith dialogue.

In the interdependent continuity of life, the hope for immortality relates to all humankind and presents the possibility of ongoing personal transformation in the context of our ongoing experience of divine revelation in all its many forms, rather than one particular pathway. Perhaps, beyond the grave when we no longer see in a glass darkly, we will discover that the God we experienced in Jesus calls us to grow in relationship to others' experiences of God in terms of the teachings of Buddha, the Upanishads, the Koran, or ancient African, American, or aboriginal wisdom. Revelation and salvation alike are evolving, with no absolute norm or form for either.

IMAGES OF IMMORTALITY

Two complementary images of immortality are at the heart of process theology's understanding of God's relationship with the world. In a world of perpetual perishing, Whitehead affirms that something of our lives must endure. Thinking of his son Eric and countless others who have died before their time, Whitehead asserts that "[i]n the inescapable flux, there is something that abides; in the overwhelming permanence, there is an element that escapes into flux."[12] Any vision of immortality we can imagine must include the poles of flux and permanence, and process and eternity. It must include the dynamic interplay of memory and possibility, characteristic of God's evolving relationship with the world. In this section, we will more fully explore two types of survival after death or immortality—*objective immortality* and *subjective immortality*, that is, the everlasting impact of our lives and the world within the divine experience and our own continuing personal adventures beyond the grave. Taken as complementary to one another, objective and subjective immortality affirm the importance of this lifetime, inspire acts of social justice, and promise hope for the future.

The Immortality of Influence. According to Whitehead, "actual entities 'perpetually perish subjectively but are immortal objectively.'

Actuality in perishing acquires objectivity, while it loses subjective immediacy."[13] In the dynamic interdependence of the universe, every moment of experience leaves it mark and has value for its successors. What it has attained in its own process of self-creation becomes its gift to the divine and creaturely future. Accordingly, what we do matters both to God and to our ongoing planetary history.

All relatedness has its foundation in the relatedness of actualities; and such relatedness is wholly concerned with the appropriation of the dead by the living—that is to say, with objective immortality; whereby what is divested of its own living immediacy becomes a real component in other immediacies of becoming. This is the doctrine that the creative advance of the world is the becoming, the perishing, and the objective immortalities of those things which jointly constitute *stubborn fact*.[14]

In the final pages of *Process and Reality,* Whitehead sees God's dynamic embrace of the world as the ultimate ground for objective immortality. Whitehead states that the flux of the universe raises the issue of "actuality with permanence, requiring fluency as its completion; and actuality with fluency, requiring permanence as its completion."[15] Whitehead further notes that:

This double problem cannot be separated into two distinct problems. Either side cannot be separated from the other. The consequent nature of God is the fluid world become 'everlasting' by its objective immortality in God. Also the objective immortality of actual occasions requires the primordial permanence of God, whereby the creative advance ever re-establishes itself endowed with the initial subjective aim derived from the relevance of God to the evolving world.[16]

Whitehead posits that God's immediate experience of our lives ensures their eternal impact of our lives in world history.

The problems of the fluency of God and the everlastingness of passing experience are solved by the same factor in the universe. This factor is the temporal world perfected by its reception and its reformation, as the fulfillment of the primordial appetition which is the basis of all order. In this way God is completed by the individual fluent satisfactions of finite fact, and the temporal occasions are completed by their everlasting union with their transformed selves, purged into conformation with the eternal order which is the final absolute 'wisdom.'[17]

Every moment of experience finds its eternity and fulfillment in God and contributes to God's future adventures in the universe. God embraces each experience *as it is* with full and complete awareness; God also experiences each moment of our lives *as it might have been* in light of God's ideal vision. God's aim at beauty for the universe ultimately shapes *how* God immortalizes us within God's life and indirectly in the ongoing life of the universe. Whitehead expresses the mysterious interplay of personal and global healing that reaches beyond the death of any particular person or moment of experience.

The wisdom of [God's] subjective aim prehends every actuality for it can be in such a perfected system—its sufferings, its sorrows, its failures, its triumphs, its immediacies of joy—woven by rightness of feeling into the harmony of universal feeling, which is always immediate, always many, always one, always with novel advance, moving onward and never perishing. The revolts of destructive evil, purely self-regarding, are dismissed into the triviality of merely individual facts; and yet the good they did achieve in individual joy, in individual sorrow, in the introduction of needed contrast, is yet saved by its relationship to the completed whole. The image—and it is but an image—the image under which this operative growth of God's nature is best conceived, is that of a tender care that nothing be lost.[18]

God's experience of the world is both objective and redemptive. Our lives perish but live forever in God's experience not just as they were but as they could have been in God's ongoing adventures of world transformation; they also become part of God's quest for greater beauty in the evolution of the universe. The "shipwrecks" of the world are recovered and repaired in God's eternally transformative experience.[19] Within God's ongoing experience, God heals all wounds and reconciles all alienation, treasuring and transforming our lives in God's everlasting life. Knowing that our efforts are treasured by God transforms our lives by giving us a sense of meaning and inspiring us to challenge injustice, persist in personal growth, and sacrifice for future generations. Our enduring impact on God's ongoing adventures responds to the "insistent craving that zest for existence be refreshed by the ever-present, unfading importance of our actions, which perish and yet live for evermore."[20] We perish as persons but our efforts at justice, beauty, and love endure in God's everlasting memory and in impact of the Divine Artistry which flows back redemptively to the temporal world.

Adventures in Immortality. The world's great religions proclaim that our current lifetime is part of holy adventure which will extend beyond the grave. In some traditions such as Hinduism, Buddhism, new spiritual movements, and esoteric Christianity, we are part of even a greater adventure in which our current life has emerged from many past incarnations and will continue indefinitely through further deaths and rebirths. However we imagine the afterlife, open-minded theologians must take the possibility of survival after death seriously and frame images of the afterlife that affirm the importance of this lifetime in light of hope for future spiritual evolution. As process theologian David Griffin asserts:

> The belief that we are on a spiritual journey, a journey in which there will be sufficient time to travel to reach our destination, can motivate us to think creatively about things we can do now, socially and even internationally as well as individually, to help ourselves move here and now toward what we should be.[21]

Process theology affirms the continuity between our present life and the afterlife in terms of life experiences, personal identity, and ethical responsibility. At death and throughout eternity, a process vision of the afterlife balances personal identity with intimate interdependence. The peace, that is, the fulfillment of the spiritual adventure, Whitehead asserts, is not the result of losing your personal identity but expanding your identity to embrace a larger universe in which the well-being of others and one's own well-being are interconnected. Survival after death widens rather than narrows the scope of our attention. Accordingly, process theology asserts that post-mortem healing and bliss is ultimately incompatible with the existence of eternal punishment for the non-elect or unbeliever. Contrary to those believers whose spiritual consolation comes from escaping the hell that awaits others, process theologians believe that for any of us to experience the fullness of life, all of us must be on the road to healing and wholeness. In this lifetime and in the afterlife, peace involves a greater sensitivity to pain and not denial or anesthesia.

Peace is the removal of inhibition and not its introduction. It results in a wider sweep of conscious interest. It enlarges the field of attention. Thus Peace is self-control at its widest,—at the width where the 'self' is lost, and interest has been transferred to coordinations wider than the personality.[22]

Contemporary physics understands energy both in terms of particles and waves. The same may be true for the ways process theologians have understood survival after death. Process theologians have imagined survival after death in two contrasting ways. Following the episodic, or particle, approach characteristic of Whitehead's understanding of actual occasions, Marjorie Suchocki sees the afterlife in terms of the transformation of occasions of experience in the context of God's ongoing inner experience, or *consequent nature*. Following a wave-like approach, which I believe is reflective of the process-relational nature of our day to day lived experience, I suggest a vision of survival after death, continuous with our lifetime, and aiming toward greater wholeness in the context of an evolving post-mortem spiritual environment. From this perspective, "the realm of God" is an interdependent and evolving community in which our creativity and freedom persist in partnership with God. The ongoing series of experiences that characterize this lifetime continue in new and adventurous ways beyond the grave. While neither Suchocki nor I discuss reincarnation, process theology's images of the afterlife can also be interpreted within a theory of reincarnation that affirms interdependence, evolution, creativity, and personal identity.

Suchocki sees survival after death in terms of personal transformation at the microcosmic level of momentary personal experience. Suchocki recognizes that an interdependent universe is the source of evil as well as good. Accordingly, the structure of relatedness characteristic of history is ambiguous and cannot ultimately provide either personal or corporate healing. In the spirit of Reinhold Niebuhr, Suchocki notes that the structure of history creates

an inescapable ambiguity with regard to good and evil, for relationality is at once the structure through which evil occurs, and the structure through which redemption occurs. Therefore, there can be no full overcoming of evil within the historical process of the world. The very nature of evil in the relationality of freedom and finitude is such that evil in principle cannot be answered fully in finite circumstances—the over-coming of evil is always partial.[23]

Each occasion of experience perishes in terms of its immediacy, but lives forever in terms of its impact on the future, both human and divine. Suchocki wonders if it might be possible for a momentary occasion of experience to somehow retain its immediacy after its process of self-creation has ended. The retention of immediacy makes it possible, Suchocki believes, for the occasion to experience redemption from ambiguity and evil by experiencing its life as part of God's process of creative transformation and redemption. Experiencing ourselves, moment by moment, as existing within God's ongoing aim at beauty allows us to experience both judgment and healing. We see our lives as they were, as they could have been, and now as healed in God's experience of each moment of experience.

Suchocki recognizes that memory without transformation may itself lead to greater pain. This surely is the case in the traditional understanding of hell as eternal punishment or judgment. As Suchocki notes, "everlasting retention of immediacy is not sufficient to constitute the overcoming of evil, and in fact could constitute an evil."[24] While the loss of immediacy is, for Whitehead, a source of pain and evil, non-existence is preferable to eternal retention of experiences of hatred, violence, injustice, and unendurable physical or mental anguish. Even though the past is complete and thus cannot be changed, Suchocki suggests that past occasions of experience can experience transformation in the immediacy of God's redemptive experience. This is a matter of grace, not creaturely creativity or effort, since God's own transformational vision is the source of healing. We live in on God and experience ourselves as God experiences us as contributing to God's evolving realm of healing, wholeness, and beauty.

Suchocki's vision of survival after death finds its inspiration in a few evocative passages from *Process and Reality*. According to Whitehead, in God's experience "there is no loss, no obstruction. The world is felt in a unison of immediacy. The property of combining creative advance with the retention of immediacy is what is meant . . . by the term 'everlasting.'"[25] Whitehead further notes that "in everlastingness immediacy is reconciled with objective immortality."[26]

God's ongoing immediacy of experience is guided by God's aim at healing and beauty. God's ongoing experience combines both objectivity and transformation of the world within God and in God's ongoing relationship with history. "God does not create the world, he saves it: or more accurately, he is the poet of the world, with tender patience leading it by his vision of truth, beauty, and goodness."[27] In God's "tender care that nothing be lost," God maintains the immediacy of historically past occasions:

> The sense of worth beyond itself is immediately enjoyed as an overpowering element in the individual self-attainment. It is in this way that the immediacy of sorrow and pain is transformed into an element of triumph. This is the notion of redemption through suffering that haunts the world.[28]

Within God's evolving experience, momentary occasions of experience, having perished in their earthly immediacy, now see themselves as they were and as they could be. No longer able to initiate new creative adventures, they are transformed solely by God's initiative, that is, by experiencing themselves in terms of God's vision. This apotheosis, or making holy, within God's experience allows the occasion to recognize its imperfections as well as possibilities for transformation and positive influence in the evolving universe as a result of God's healing love. In Suchocki's vision of survival after death, "in the apotheosis, the finite satisfaction remains itself even while it experiences God's transforming power."[29] God's healing and transformation of the past expands the momentary occasion's sense of itself and its relationship to the world. Within God's experience, a human being, for example, experiences each moment of her or his life in terms of the whole of her life and the world around her. As Suchocki notes, "The occasion is 'saved by its relation to the completed whole' (PR 346). The immediacy of the occasion is then both itself and others, both one and many, both finite and infinite in the ultimate togetherness which is God."[30] Transformation occurs, in Suchocki's vision, by creaturely observation and not further subjective self-creation; for the creature is unable to take any new initiatives in self-creation. In experiencing God's freedom and vision, we experience our beatification. We cannot change the past or create future experiences, but the redemptive power of everlasting life involves God's transformation and healing of the past—our past experiences one by one and in their entirety—within God's own experience.

In the following paragraphs, I will suggest an alternative, stream or wave-like, understanding of survival after death. While I am highly appreciative of Suchocki's creative post-mortem vision, I want to take it a step further in the spirit of Whitehead's metaphysics of creativity, interdependence, and divine inspiration. The key issue involves whether or not our afterlife consists of an ongoing stream of creative experiences, similar to and emerging from our current experience, following our physical death. Does the stream of experience end at physical death, and with it our personal creativity and freedom? Or do these values continue, along with greater interdependence, growth, and adventure beyond the grave? Do we create new experiences that add new data and possibilities for God, others, and ourselves in the afterlife? My own approach is influenced by an integration of Whitehead's metaphysics, universalistic understandings of the afterlife and resurrection, and the evidence of near death and paranormal experiences. I believe that process theology invites us to imagine a more abundant, rather than less abundant, life beyond the grave. The afterlife awakens us to greater and more vital opportunities for transformation, freedom, and creativity. Beyond the grave, we continue to grow in wisdom, stature, and openness to the divine.

Any understanding of survival after death from a process perspective must take into account the realities of relationship, memory, and novelty characteristic of this lifetime. Within this lifetime, personal identity from a process perspective involves an ever-flowing stream of experiences in which the past is: 1) preserved, consciously and unconsciously, 2) embraced as objectively immortal in shaping the present moment of experience, and 3) transformed in the immediacy present experience in light of the call of the future. Within the present moment's inheritance and transformation of the past is both the energy of the stream of experiences itself as it moves from past to future and the ever-present creative wisdom of God, whose vision weaves together each momentary experience into the emerging and evolving self. As I discussed earlier, process theology sees selfhood as dynamic and relational; there is no unchanging substance under girding our experiences, rather the process of moment by moment arising and perishing and aiming toward the future constitutes who we are and what we will become. Though shaped by the impact of environment, past decisions, and divine inspiration, the self in this life and beyond the grave emerges moment by moment through its decisions to creatively synthesize these factors in its own unique way. Although the stream can be described as a series of moments, nevertheless, continuity, rather than episodic individuality, characterizes our lived human experience.

This same continuity propels the self forward at the moment of death. The God who was present in the energy of conception is equally present at the moment of death, luring us forward as God has done from the beginning toward the next adventure in partnership with God and the world. My approach sees life beyond the grave as lively, creative, and adventurous. We are neither absolutely transformed, that is, perfected at death; nor are we frozen in eternal damnation or passive life review. Our lives will receive new energy and new possibility for growing in grace and relationship with God and one another. We will continue to be artists of our experience, growing toward God and others through our moment by moment decisions.

In the spirit of the later Hebraic and early Christian experiences, I believe that the afterlife is profoundly relational in nature. The afterlife is not characterized by individualistic isolation as some suggest, but relational living and acting in the context of an evolving community. Beyond the grave, process theology suggests that we will continue to experience interactive relationships as a source of insight, growth, and challenge. We may have the opportunity within God's realm of wholeness and Shalom to experience the pain we caused, or that was inflicted on us, in such a way that healing and reconciliation are promoted for us and others. We may, as the Apostle Paul suggests in I Corinthians 13:12, "know as we are known."

Personal identity does not end at death, but continues in an environment which nurtures freedom, creativity, growth, and relationship with God and others. Here, the insights of some versions of purgatory and reincarnation may be helpful in articulating a process-relational vision of the afterlife. Taken as a metaphor, purgatory suggests that our journey toward God is incomplete at the moment of death, but will be completed through our post-mortem encounters with God. Our personal growth in relationship with God requires that we let go of everything that has kept us from following God's vision and experiencing God's abundant life. We need to forgive and be forgiven if we are to more fully experience the realm of God as the goal of our lives. Taken as a metaphor, reincarnation, like purgatory, is a reminder that we reap what we sow and that the influence past must be addressed, accepted, and healed in any future lifetime. From a process perspective, the energy described in the doctrine of reincarnation moves people forward in such a way that they have opportunities to make amends for past mistakes and eventually discover their true identity. As metaphors for our post-mortem journeys, purgatory and reincarnation aim toward wholeness and communion with the ultimate reality.

The afterlife vision I suggest goes beyond traditional and literal understandings of purgatory and resurrection in its affirmation that God's relationship continues to be intimate, variable, and constant for all people beyond the grave. God is at work within our lives with greater immediacy and intensity so that our future decisions more fully reflect God's vision of who we can be in this community of love. Still, in the spirit of process theology, we will continue to grow, learn new things, explore new possibilities, and chart new adventures. We will not be passive in our afterlife, but creators along with God of our future and the realm of Shalom. In the afterlife, we still possess an element of freedom and self-determination that allows us to respond to God's vision in our own unique and surprising way. God's inspiration will continue to address us uniquely in light of our history, gifts, and personality. The realm of God will be a place of greater, rather than lesser, creativity, artistry, exploration, and diversity in which we may come to fully know our evolving role in the "body of Christ."

Process theology's affirmation of universal revelation begs the question: "Where do other faith traditions and visions of salvation fit in?" Thus far, my vision of survival after death has primarily reflected the insights of Christian theology, albeit in a transformed and expanded form. Process theology's recognition of the continuity of this life and the next suggests that persons enter the afterlife with their own culturally and religiously formed visions of immortality that will shape their post-mortem experience. If there is no absolute uniformity in this lifetime, can we expect or desire absolute uniformity in the afterlife? Perhaps, and it is a great perhaps, that as persons evolve in the afterlife, they will come to know a multidimensional God who invites them to experience reality in many different ways, embracing and going beyond the wisdom of the great faith traditions. Perhaps, we will grow in our awareness and experience of the many-faceted God through post-mortem encounters with other religious traditions and their savior figures. In the dynamics of post-mortem existence, some persons may discover God in terms of "the drop of water returning to the ocean," while others may experience the afterlife as synergistic community in which we grow to become Christ-like in our loving embrace of the universe. Our experiences beyond the grave may begin where we left off at the moment of death, as we initially interpret the our post-mortem experience in terms of our current religious symbols, and then grow in dialogue with others and in relationship with God toward more inclusive and dynamic images of the afterlife.

Further, my vision of the afterlife also begs the question, "Where do we draw the line in terms of the scope of immortality in terms of human and non-human life?" If non-humans also experience themselves as conscious and, to some extent, creative, "Will members of many of the earth's species continue to evolve after death? Will they live in their own species world, or share a common world with us?" Clearly, all creatures will live on God's memory in terms of objective immortality, but is this enough to claim for higher organisms, such as dolphins and chimpanzees? Here, we are entering a realm that stretches our imaginations, especially if we anticipate that the universe is teeming with life beyond our solar system and galaxy. In a universe of innumerable galaxies, we can only imagine the many ways that God will continue to address the world and its diverse creatures in this life and the next. Process theology has no precise eschatological vision as it relates to non-humans, both less and more evolved than ourselves, but it honors the imaginative quest to push the boundaries of theology, spirituality, and ethics to embrace the possibility of many diverse and surprising images of the afterlife.

CHAPTER 10

NEW HORIZONS FOR PROCESS THEOLOGY

Today, Christian faith is in search of a convincing, yet humble, vision of reality. Postmodern thinkers deny the possibility of any universal theology or metaphysic in favor of personal and tribal stories. While it is clear that all theology is contextual and socially-located, this limitation should not prevent theologians from articulating theological visions that join a global perspective with the concreteness of personal experience. John Cobb asserted in his challenging text, *Reclaiming the Church: Where the Mainline Church Went Wrong and What to Do about It,* that the primary obstacle to congregational and denominational renewal is "the inability of the church to think theologically."[1] Inspired by Cobb's diagnosis, I believe that only innovative and imaginative visions of the relationship between theology and everyday life can provide the inspiration for congregational and personal transformation in the postmodern world.

Among the culprits in the irrelevance of theology to daily life and political involvement has been the modern world's emphasis on professional specialization and the compartmentalization of academic disciplines. In the quest for scientific clarity, whether in medicine or theology, professionals have lost touch with the whole person and her or his lived experience. Whereas Western medicine often confused the medical chart in its abstraction for the living person in all of her or his concrete complexity, theologians have often crafted complex systems in isolation from the initial mystical experiences and questions of faith from which theological reflection initially emerged. In the world of academic theology, practitioners have been viewed as inferior to academics and emotion and intuition as inferior to thought. The experiences of lay persons have been discounted as of little value in theological reflection. In this context, Philip Clayton calls for a "rebirth of theology" as a partnership between academics, laypeople, and clergy. Theology, according to Clayton, must reclaim its role as holistic discipline, related to every aspect of lived experience and committed to the mission of the church. Clayton contends that "it's *my* responsibility as a theologian to help draw connections to the life of the church, and this responsibility cannot be shunted off on others."[2] Clayton challenges his professional colleagues to become partners with laypeople and clergy in transforming Christian theology.

Process theology is by orientation transformational and visionary. Forward looking in nature, process theology sees the theological task as ultimately experiential, holistic, and relational. While the language of process theology has often been an impediment in its impact on the lives and vocations of laypeople and clergy, a transformed process theology can be preached, taught, and lived in ways that transform people and communities. When process theology is truly experienced—and lived—by its practitioners, it fulfills its promise as an experience-based, open-ended, and spiritually-transformational theological movement.

In an age of theological pluralism in which pastors and theologians alike are reticent about whole-heartedly claiming a particular theological world-view, process theology seeks to present a constructive vision of Christian theology for the twenty first century, capable of addressing the intellectual challenges of the postmodern world. In both Europe and North America, throngs of Christians of all ages have abandoned traditional and conservative as well as mainstream forms of Christianity. Some have become spiritual orphans, lacking any community to call their spiritual home. Others have become part of the amorphous, yet dynamic emerging or emergent Christianity movement. In many ways, these theological adventurers represent a "new kind of Christianity," as Brian McLaren asserts, that goes beyond the polarization of doctrine and experience, this world and eternal life, non-Christians and Christians, traditional and contemporary, ritual and innovation, and social action and contemplation.[3] Still, emerging Christianity in North America, Britain, Australia, and New Zealand is in search of a unifying and integrative, yet flexible and humble theological vision, to serve as a guidepost for spiritual seekers. Faith cannot live entirely by deconstructive postmodernism or apophatic spirituality. Faith finds a flexible foundation in the humble affirmation and healing embodiment of its symbols and language in daily life. Apart from a fluid world view that embraces and transcends individual experience, emerging Christianity can become the captive of personal experience alone or the spiritual fad of the day. Process theology's holistic vision and openness to creative transformation may serve as one source of guidance for passionate refugees from conservative Christianity in their quest for a "good enough" world view and vision of God. Process theology provides an integrative vision, joining order and novelty, and ancient and contemporary, for persons seeking new ways of being Christian.

Cobb appropriately recognizes that the failure to take theology seriously has led to the growing irrelevance of moderate and progressive Christianity in the larger society. Healthy theology gives people a pathway to face tragedy, social change, and injustice with a sense of hope and empowerment. Process theology's vision of the open-endedness of life in concert with its vision of lively divine companionship and creativity provides both inspiration and encouragement for courageous commitment to social transformation and planetary renewal. But, theology alone cannot save or inspire us. Theology must be expanded and envisaged to embrace the whole person, body, mind, and spirit. Vital faith must be a matter of heart and hands as well as head. Christian convictions need to be under girded and enlivened by spiritual practices. Here process theology provides resources for spiritual seekers that can heal and transform mind, body, and spirit. Process theology can be experienced as well as discussed. If God is truly omnipresent, touching each moment with new and lively possibilities, then our spiritual practices can awaken us to God's movements toward beauty and wholeness in our personal and corporate commitments. In its experiential orientation and whole-person approach to life, process theology unites action and contemplation, and embodiment and intellect, in the quest for justice and planetary healing.

The twenty first century cries out for insightful, earth-affirming, and pluralistic theologies. Although we cannot claim too much for any theological vision, including process theology, it is clear that consumerism, materialism, and other-worldliness have had disastrous effects on economics, equality, and the environment.[4] At the very least, flexible theological visions, such as that proposed by process theology, can fulfill the mandate of both medicine and theological reflection, "first do no harm." But, more than that, the new horizons for process theology involve providing pathways toward appreciation and celebration of diversity, pluralism, creativity, wholeness of mind, body, and spirit, and healing the earth. In so doing, process theology invites people to go beyond the individualistic ego to experience the peace that comes from world loyalty and the recognition that our efforts to heal the earth are inspired and treasured by God in this moment and forevermore.

NOTES

ACKNOWLEDGMENTS

1 Alfred North Whitehead, *Religion in the Making* (New York: Meridian Books, 1972), 15.

CHAPTER 1

1 Alfred North Whitehead, *Religion in the Making*, 16.
2 John B. Cobb, *Whitehead Word Book* (Claremont, CA: P&F Press, 2008).
3 Alan Jones in the preface to Margaret Guenther's *Holy Listening: The Art of Spiritual Direction* (Cambridge: Cowley, 1992), x.
4 Rick Warren, *Purpose Driven Life: What on Earth am I Here For?* (Grand Rapids, MI: Zondervan, 2002), 21.
5 Ibid., 194.
6 Ibid., 69–76.
7 Ibid., 194–198.
8 Tim LaHaye, *Left Behind* (Carol Stream, IL: Tyndale House, 1996).
9 Brian Greene, *The Elegant Universe: Superstrings, Hidden Dimensions, and the Quest for Ultimate Theory* (New York: Vintage Books, 2000).
10 Alfred North Whitehead, *Process and Reality: Corrected Edition*, 208.
11 Ibid., 208.
12 Ibid., 338.
13 Ibid., 209.
14 Victor Lowe, *Alfred North Whitehead: The Man and His Work*, Volume I: 1861–1910 (Baltimore, MD: The Johns Hopkins University Press, 1985), 188.
15 Ibid., 5.
16 Ibid., 5.
17 Whitehead, *Science and the Modern World* (New York: Free Press, 1967), 191–192.
18 Victor Lowe, *Alfred North Whitehead: The Man and His Work, Volume II: 1910–1947*, edited by J.B. Shneewind (Baltimore, MD: The Johns Hopkins University Press, 1990), 188.
19 John B. Cobb, *Whitehead Word Book* (Claremont, CA: P&F Press, 2008), 7.
20 Victor Lowe, vol. 2, 250.

21 Lucien Price, *The Dialogues of Whitehead* (Boston, MA: Little, Brown and Company, 1954), 370–371.

22 For a concise, yet comprehensive summary of the academic careers of the major process theologians, see Gary Dorrien, *The Making of American Liberal Theology: Crisis, Irony, and Postmodernity, 1950–2005* (Louisville, KY: Westminster/John Knox, 2006), 58–132, 190–268.

23 A brief summary of Charles Hartshorne's philosophy can be found in David Wayne Viney, "Charles Hartshorne," in Michael Weber and Will Desmond, *Handbook of Whiteheadian Process Thought*, volume two, (Frankfort, Germany: OntosVerlag, 2008), 589–596.

24 For a brief summary of Loomer's theology see Bruce Epperly, "Bernard M. Loomer" in *Handbook of Whiteheadian Process Thought*, volume 2, 604–608.

25 For a brief summary of Cobb's theology, see Paul CustodioBube, "John Cobb" in *Handbook of Whiteheadian Process Thought,* volume 2, 571–579.

26 John B. Cobb, *Can Christ Become Good News Again?* (St. Louis, MO: Chalice Press, 1991), 8.

27 Ibid., 9.

28 For a brief summary of Griffin's work, see Bruce Epperly, "David Griffin" in *Handbook of Whiteheadian Process Thought*, volume 2, 583–586.

29 For more on the Center for Process Studies, see www.ctr4process.org

30 www.processandfaith.org

31 Marjorie Suchocki, *What is Process Theology? Conversations with Marjorie* (Claremont, CA: P&F Press, 2003), 4.

32 *Process and Reality: Corrected Edition,* 3.

33 Ibid., 5.

34 Ibid., 8.

35 Ibid., 9.

36 Robert Mesle, *Process-Relational Philosophy: An Introduction to Alfred North Whitehead* (West Conshohocken, PA: John Templeton Press) 12.

37 Ibid., xiv.

38 Ibid., 15–16.

39 Whitehead, *Religion in the Making,* 30–33.

40 Rene Descartes describes a substance as follows: "By substance, we can understand nothing else than a thing which so exists that it needs no other thing in order to exist." In Rene Descartes, *Philosophical Works of Descartes,* Volume 1, trans. Elizabeth Haldane and G.R.T. Ross (New York: Dover, 1931), 232.

41 Ibid., p. 18.

42 Larry Dossey, *Space, Time, and Medicine* (Boulder, CO: Shambala, 1992); Bruce Epperly, *God's Touch: Faith, Wholeness, and the Healing Miracles of Jesus* (Louisville, KY: Westminster/John Knox, 2005); Dale Matthews, *The Faith Factor: The Proof of the Healing Power of Prayer* (New York: Penguin, 1999); Candace Pert, *The Molecules of Emotion* (New York: Simon and Schuster, 1995).

43 C. Robert Mesle, *Process-Relational Philosophy: An Introduction to Alfred North Whitehead*, 38.

44 Ronald Farmer, *Awakening* (Scots Valley, CA: Create Space, 2009).
45 See also Psalm 148–150.
46 Robert Frost, "A Considerable Speck."
47 Jean-Pierre de Caussade, *The Sacrament of the Present Moment* (New York: Harper San Francisco, 1989).
48 Rick Warren, *The Purpose Driven Life* (Grand Rapids, MI: Zondervan, 2002).
49 Victor Frankl, *From Death Camp to Existentialism* (Boston, MA: Beacon Press, 1959), 65.
50 Process and Reality, 343.
51 Ibid., 7.
52 Robert Neville, *Creativity and God: A Challenge to Process Theology* (New York: Seabury Press, 1980).
53 Whitehead, *Process and Reality*, 212.
54 Ibid., 21.
55 Whitehead, *Religion in the Making*, 147.

CHAPTER 2

1 Charles Hartshorne, *The Divine Relativity: A Social Conception of God* (New Haven, CT: Yale University Press, 1948), x.
2 Terence Fretheim, *The Suffering of God: An Old Testament Perspective,* (Philadelphia, PA: Westminster Press, 1984), 1.
3 Whitehead, *Religion in the Making*, 15.
4 Ibid., 16.
5 For a fictional exploration of the role of our images of God in personal transformation, see Patricia Adams Farmer's *The Metaphor Maker* (Scots Valley, CA: Estrella de Mar Publications, 2009).
6 John B. Cobb, *God and the World* (Philadelphia, PA: Westminster Press, 1969), 42.
7 Whitehead, *Process and Reality,* 102.
8 Aristotle, *Metaphysics* 1074b. Translated by W.D. Ross and J.A. Smith, *The Works of Aristotle* (Oxford: Clarendon Press, 1917).
9 Anselm, *Proslogium.* Translated by S.N. Deane (La Salle, IL: Open Court, 1945), 13–14.
10 Thomas Jay Oord, *The Nature of Love: A Theology* (St. Louis, MO: Chalice Press, 2010), 15.
11 Whitehead, *Process and Reality,* 342.
12 Oord, *The Nature of Love,* 5.
13 Rick Warren, *The Purpose Driven Life* (Grand Rapids, MI: Zondervan, 2002), 9.
14 Ibid., 21.
15 Ibid., 22–23.
16 Ibid., 23.
17 Ibid., 42–43.
18 Ibid., 194.
19 Ibid., 195–196.
20 Ibid., 196.

21 Charles Hartshorne, "Ethics and the New Theology," *The International Journal of Ethics* 15:1 (October 1934), 97.

22 Bruce Epperly, *Holy Adventure: 41 Days of Audacious Living* (Nashville, TN: Upper Room, 2008).

23 John B. Cobb and David Ray Griffin, *Process Theology: An Introductory Exposition* (Louisville, KY: Westminster/John Knox, 1976).

24 Hartshorne, *The Divine Relativity,* xvii

25 Whitehead, *Religion in the Making, 147.*

26 Whitehead, *Process and Reality,* 224.

27 Ibid., 244.

28 Ibid., 244.

29 Ibid., 351.

30 Whitehead, *Religion in the Making,* 153.

31 Whitehead, *Adventures of Ideas,* 265.

32 Whitehead, *Process and Reality,* 346.

33 Ibid., 346.

34 Charles Hartshorne, *The Divine Relativity,* 30.

35 William Blake, *Songs of Innocence and of Experience* (New York: The Orion Press, 1967), 27.

36 Ibid., 346.

37 Martin Luther, quoted in David Ray Griffin *God, Power, and Evil: A Process Theodicy* (London: Westminster/John Knox, 2004), 103.

38 John Calvin, *Institutes of the Christian Religion,* edited by John T. McNeill, translated by Lewis Ford Battles, Volumes XX and XXI of the *Library Christian Classics* (Philadelphia, PA: Westminster Press, 1960), I, xvi, 5–6.

39 Griffin, *God, Power, and Evil,* 279–280.

40 Ibid., 286.

41 Ibid., 291.

42 Ibid., 294.

43 Whitehead, *Process and Reality,* 351.

44 See the following texts: *Spirituality and Health: Health and Spirituality* (Mystic, CT: Twenty-third Publications, 1997); *God's Touch: Faith, Wholeness, and the Healing Miracles of Jesus* (Louisville, KY: Westminster/ John Knox, 2001); *Walking in the Light: Jewish-Christian Visions of Healing and Wholeness* (St. Louis, MO: Chalice Press, 2004); *Reiki Healing Touch and the Way of Jesus* (Kelowna, BC: Northstone Press, 2005); and *Healing Worship: Purpose and Practice* (Cleveland, OH: Pilgrim Press, 2006).

45 Marjorie Suchocki, *In God's Presence: Theological Reflections on Prayer* (St. Louis, MO: Chalice Press, 1996), 4.

46 Ibid., 5.

47 Ibid., 18.

48 Ibid., 18.

49 Ibid., 28.

50 Ibid., 46, 47.

51 Ibid., 52.

NOTES

CHAPTER 3

1 Alfred North Whitehead, *Adventures in Ideas*, 167.
2 Whitehead, *Process and Reality*, 343.
3 John Cobb, *Can Christ Become Good News Again?* (St. Louis, MO: Chalice Press, 1991).
4 David Ray Griffin, *A Process Christology* (Philadelphia, PA: Westminster Press, 1973), 20.
5 Ibid., 180.
6 Whitehead, *Religion in the Making*, 149.
7 John Cobb, *Christ in a Pluralistic Age* (Philadelphia, PA: Westminster Press, 1975), 171.
8 Some examples of process theologians in dialogue with other religions include: John B. Cobb, *Beyond Dialogue: Toward a Mutual Transformation of Buddhism and Christianity* (Minneapolis, MN: Fortress Press, 1982; Bruce Epperly, *Reiki Healing Touch and the Way of Jesus* (Kelowna, BC:Northstone Press, 2005); Jay McDaniel, *Gandhi's Truth: Learning from the World's Religions as a Path Toward Peace* (New York: Orbis Press, 2005); Marjorie Suchocki, *Divinity and Diversity: A Christian Affirmation of Religious Pluralism* (Nashville, TN: Abingdon Press, 2003).
9 Griffin, *A Process Christology*, 209.
10 Ibid., 215.
11 Ibid., 216.
12 Marjorie Suchocki, *God, Christ, Church*, 95–96.
13 Clark Williamson, *A Guest in the House of Israel: Post-Holocaust Church Theology* (Louisville, KY: Westminster/John Knox, 1993).
14 John Cobb and David Ray Griffin, *Process Theology: An Introductory Exposition*, 105.
15 Ibid., 105.
16 Cobb, *Christ in a Pluralistic Age*, 84, 89
17 For more on Jesus as healer, see Bruce Epperly *God's Touch: Faith, Wholeness, and the Healing Miracles of Jesus* (Louisville, KY: Westminster/John Knox, 2001) and *Healing Worship: Purpose and Practice* (Cleveland, OH: Pilgrim Press,2006), and Rita Nakashima Brock, *Journeys by Heart: A Christology of Erotic Power* (New York: Crossroad, 1988).
18 See Bruce Epperly, *Reiki Healing Touch and the Way of Jesus* (Kelowna, BC: Northstone, 2005).
19 Whitehead, *Process and Reality*, 351.
20 For a sustained critique of substitutionary atonement, see Rita Nakashima Brock and Rebecca Ann Parker, *Proverbs of Ashes* (Boston, MA: Beacon Press, 2002)and *Saving Paradise* (Boston, MA: Beacon Press, 2009).
21 Suchocki, *God, Christ, Church*, 106.
22 Suchocki, *God, Christ, Church*, 111.
23 Ibid., 112.
24 Cobb and Griffin, *Process Theology: An Introductory Exposition*, 99.
25 Ibid., 102.
26 Ibid., 102.

CHAPTER 4

1 John Cobb, *Is It Too Late? A Theology of Ecology* (Beverly Hills, CA: Bruce, 1971), 143–144.
2 Marjorie Suchocki, *God-Christ-Church*, 213.
3 John Cobb and David Griffin, *Process Theology: An Introductory Exposition*, 110.
4 Ibid., 109.
5 Ibid., 110.
6 Lewis Ford, "Contingent Transcendence." In Joseph Bracken and Marjorie Suchocki, *Trinity in Process* (Lexington, NY: Continuum, 1997), 44.
7 Marjorie Suchocki, "Spirit in and Through the World." Ibid., 182.
8 Ibid., 183–184.
9 Norman Pittenger, *The Holy Spirit* (Philadelphia, PA: Pilgrim Press, 1974), 17.
10 Ibid., 65.
11 Karen Baker-Fletcher, *Dancing with God: The Trinity in a Womanist Perspective* (St. Louis, MO: Chalice, 2006), 19.
12 Teilhard de Chardin, *The Prayer of the Universe* (New York: Harper and Row, 1973).
13 Marjorie Suchocki, *Trinity in Process*, x.
14 Ibid., 10–11.
15 Marjorie Suchocki, *Divinity and Diversity*, 67.
16 Marjorie Suchocki, *God-Christ-Church*, 213.
17 Ibid., 213.

CHAPTER 5

1 Alfred North Whitehead, *Modes of Thought* (New York: Free Press, 1968), 21.
2 Alfred North Whitehead, *Adventures of Ideas* (New York: Free Press, 1963), 296.
3 Ian Barbour, *Religion in an Age of Science* (New York: Harper San Francisco, 1990), 191.
4 John Cobb, *A Christian Natural Theology*, 19.
5 Ibid., 24.
6 Bruce Epperly, *At the Edges of Life: A Holistic Vision of the Human Adventure* (St. Louis, MO: Chalice Press, 1992), revised from 27–28.
7 Alfred North Whitehead, *Modes of Thought*, 26.
8 Ibid., 28.
9 For a more detailed reflection the relationship of process theology to issues of health and illness and the healings of Jesus, see Bruce Epperly, *At the Edges of Life: A Holistic Vision of the Human Adventure* (St. Louis, MO: Chalice Press, 1992) and *God's Touch: Faith, Wholeness, and the Healing Miracles of Jesus* (Louisville, KY: Westminster/John Knox, 2001).
10 John Cobb, *The Structure of Christian Existence* (Philadelphia, NY: Westminster Press, 1969).
11 Helene Russell, *Iragary and Kierkegaard: On the Construction of the Self* (Macon, GA: Mercer University Press, 2009).

12 Alfred North Whitehead, *Religion in the Making*, 57.
13 Alfred North Whitehead, *Adventures in Ideas*, 285.
14 Whitehead, *Adventures of Ideas*, 273–283.
15 Marjorie Suchocki, *God-Christ-Church*, 22.
16 Ibid., 25.
17 Marjorie Suchocki, *Fall to Violence: Original Sin in a Relational Theology* (New York: Continuum, 1995), 12.
18 Suchocki, *Fall to Violence*, 16.
19 Ibid., 60.
20 Helene Russell, *Iragary and Kierkegaard*, 254.
21 Ibid., 3.
22 Whitehead, *Process and Reality*, 244.

CHAPTER 6

1 Alfred North Whitehead, *Science and the Modern World*, 189.
2 Ibid., 34.
3 Ian Barbour, *Religion in an Age of Science* (New York: Harper San Francisco, 1990, 3–30). John Haught suggests a similar typology in *Science and Religion: From Conflict to Conversation* (New York: Paulist, 1993), 9–23. Haught's fourfold understanding of the relationship of science and religion includes: conflict, contrast, contact, and conformation.
4 John Polkinghorne, *Quarks, Chaos, and Creation* (New York: Crossroads, 1998), xi.
5 John Polkinghorne, *Traffic in Truth: Exchanges Between Science and Theology* (Minneapolis, MN: Fortress Press, 2000), 3.
6 John Cobb and David Griffin, *Process Theology: An Introductory Exposition*, 94.
7 Alfred North Whitehead, *The Function of Reason*, 7.
8 Ibid., 8.
9 Ibid., 13.
10 Ibid., 16.
11 Ibid., 25.
12 Ibid., 28.
13 Ibid., 34.
14 John Haught, *The Cosmic Adventure: Science, Religion, and the Quest for Purpose* (Mahwah, NY: Paulist Press, 1984), 3.
15 Ian Barbour, *Religion in an Age of Science*, 189–190.
16 David Ray Griffin, *God, Power, and Evil: A Process Theodicy* (Louisville, KY: Westminster/John Knox, 2004), 292.
17 Ibid., 394.
18 Ibid., 395.
19 Whitehead, *Process and Reality*, 105.

CHAPTER 7

1 Alfred North Whitehead, *Modes of Thought* (New York: Free Press, 1966), 13–14.

NOTES

2 Whitehead, *Religion in the Making*, 15.
3 John B. Cobb, *Matters of Life and Death* (Louisville, KY: Westminster/ John Knox, 1991), 9.
4 Whitehead, *Modes of Thought*, 15.
5 Ibid., 22.
6 Whitehead, *Religion in the Making*, 152.
7 Whitehead, *Modes of Thought*, 14.
8 Cobb, *Matters of Life and Death*, 73.
9 Cobb, *Matters of Life and Death*, 69.
10 Ibid., 69.
11 Ibid., 70.
12 Ronald Farmer provides a strong description for the pain experienced by animals in factory farm settings in his process-oriented novel, *Awakening* (Scots Valley, CA: Create Space, 2009).
13 Cobb, *Matters of Life and Death*, 77.
14 Cobb, *Matters of Life and Death*, 73.
15 Ibid., 89.
16 Whitehead, *Function of Reason*, 8.
17 Cobb, *Matters of Life and Death*, 44.
18 Ibid., 56.
19 Charles Birch and John Cobb, *The Liberation of Life* (Cambridge: Cambridge University Press, 1981), 141.
20 Ibid., 147.
21 Jay McDaniel, *Of God and Pelicans: A Theology of Reverence of Life* (Louisville, KY: Westminster/John Knox Press, 1989), 22.
22 Ibid., 22.
23 Ibid., 52.
24 Ibid., 79.
25 Birch and Cobb, *The Liberation of Life*, 153.
26 Birch and Cobb, *The Liberation of Life*, 151.
27 Jay McDaniel, "A Process Approach to Ecology," in Donna Bowman and Jay McDaniel, editors, *A Handbook of Process Theology* (St. Louis, MO: Chalice, 2006), 229.
28 Ibid., 245.
29 Herman Daly and John Cobb, *For the Common Good: Redirecting the Economy toward Community, the Environment, and a Sustainable Future* (Boston, MA: Beacon Press, 1989), 355.
30 John Cobb, *Sustaining the Common Good: A Christian Perspective on the Global Economy* (Cleveland, OH: Pilgrim Press, 1994), 11.
31 Karen Baker-Fletcher, *Sisters of Dust, Sisters of Spirit: Womanist Wordings on God and Creation* (Minneapolis, MN: Fortress Press, 1998), 55.
32 Ibid., 62–63.
33 Jay McDaniel, *Living from the Center: Spirituality in an Age of Consumerism* (St. Louis, MO: Chalice Press, 2000), 42, 48.
34 John Cobb, *Sustaining the Common Good*, 21, 22.
35 Monica Coleman, *Making a Way*, 78.
36 Karen Baker-Fletcher, *Sisters of Dust, Sisters of Spirit*, 58.
37 Ibid., 36.

NOTES

CHAPTER 8

1 Alfred North Whitehead, *Science and the Modern World* (New York: Macmillan, 1953), 186, 189.
2 Whitehead, *Process and Reality*, 102.
3 Larry Axel and William Dean, eds., *The Size of God: The Theology of Bernard Loomer in Context* (Macon, GA: Mercer University Press, 1987).
4 Whitehead, *Science and the Modern World*, 186.
5 Catherine Keller, *On the Mystery: Discerning God in Process* (Minneapolis, MN: Fortress Press, 2008), 2–3.
6 Ibid., 14.
7 Russell Pregeant, "Scripture and Revelation." In Donna Bowman and Jay McDaniel, *Handbook of Process Theology* (St. Louis, MO: Chalice Press, 2006), 67.
8 For more detailed expressions of process spirituality, see Marjorie Suchocki, *In God's Presence: Theological Reflections on Prayer* (St. Louis, MO: Chalice, 1996); Jay McDaniel. *Living from the Center: Spirituality in an Age of Consumerism* (St. Louis, MO: Chalice, 2000); Bruce Epperly *Holy Adventure: Forty One Days of Audacious Living* (Nashville, TN: Upper Room, 2008), *The Power of Affirmative Faith*(St. Louis: Chalice, 2000), and *Tending to the Holy: The Practice of the Presence of God in Ministry* (Herndon, VA: Alban Institute, 2008); and Patricia Adams Farmer, *Embracing a Beautiful God* (St. Louis, MO: Chalice, 2003).
9 Malcolm Muggeridge, *Something Beautiful for God: The Classic Account of Mother Teresa's Journey into Compassion* (New York: Harper One, 1986).
10 Lisa Withrow, *Claiming New Life: Process-Church for the Future* (St. Louis, MO: Chalice Press,2009), 2.
11 Suchocki, *God-Christ-Church*, 206.
12 Monica Coleman, *Making a Way Out of Now Way: A Womanist Theology* (Minneapolis, MN: Fortress, 2008).
13 William A. Beardslee, *A House for Hope: A Study in Process and Biblical Thought* (Philadelphia, PA: Westminster Press, 1972), 172.
14 William A. Beardslee, "Hope in Biblical Eschatology and Process Theology," *Journal of the American Academy of Religion* 38 (1970), 238. Quoted in Ronald L. Farmer, *Beyond the Impasse: The Promise of a Process Hermeneutic* (Macon, GA: Mercer University Press, 1997), 198.
15 Ronald Farmer, *Beyond the Impasse*, 198.
16 Clark Williamson, *A Guest in the House of Israel* (Louisville, MO: Westminster/John Knox, 1993) and *When Jews and Christians Meet* (St. Louis: CBP Press, 1989).

CHAPTER 9

1 Alfred North Whitehead, *Adventures of Ideas*, 296.
2 Monica A. Coleman, *Making a Way Out of No Way: A Womanist Theology*, 94.
3 Whitehead, *Religion in the Making*, 107.
4 John B. Cobb, *A Christian Natural Theology*, 35.

167

5 Coleman, *Making a Way Out of No Way,* 169.
6 Whitehead, *The Function of Reason,* 8.
7 Marjorie Suchocki, *Divinity and Diversity: A Christian Understanding of Religious Pluralism* (Nashville, TN: Abingdon Press, 2003), 57.
8 Ibid., 40.
9 Jay McDaniel, *Gandhi's Hope: Learning from other Religions as a Path to Peace,* 5.
10 Ibid., 9.
11 Charles A. Miles, "In the Garden."
12 Whitehead, *Process and Reality,* 338.
13 Ibid., 29.
14 Ibid., xiii–xiv.
15 Ibid., 347.
16 Ibid., 347.
17 Ibid., 347.
18 Ibid., 346.
19 Ibid., 346.
20 Ibid., 351.
21 David Ray Griffin, *Parapsychology, Philosophy, and Spirituality: A Postmodern Exploration* (Albany: State University of New York Press, 1997), 291.
22 Alfred North Whitehead, *Adventures in Ideas,* 285.
23 Marjorie Suchocki, *The End of Evil: Process Eschatology in Historical Context* (Albany: State University of New York Press, 1988), 81.
24 Suchocki, *The End of Evil,* 97.
25 Whitehead, *Process and Reality,* 346.
26 Ibid., 351.
27 Ibid., 346.
28 Ibid., 350.
29 Suchocki, *The End of Evil,* 102.
30 *The End of Evil,* 106.

CHAPTER 10

1 John Cobb, *Reclaiming the Church: Where the Mainline Church Went Wrong and What to Do about It* (Louisville, KY: Westminster/John Knox, 1997), 5.
2 Philip Clayton, *Transforming Christian Theology: For Church and Society* (Minneapolis, MN: AugsburgFortress, 2010), 5.
3 Brian McLaren, *A New Kind of Christianity* (San Francisco: Harper One, 2010).
4 For a spiritual response to consumerism and ecological destruction, see Jay McDaniel, *Living from the Center: Spirituality in an Age of Consumerism* (St. Louis, MO: Chalice, 2000).

SELECTED BIBLIOGRAPHY

Allen, Ronald and Clark Williamson, *A Credible and Timely Word* (St. Louis: Chalice Press, 1991).

Axel, Larry and William Dean, eds., *The Size of God: The Theology of Bernard Loomer in Context* (Macon, GA: Mercer University Press, 1987).

Baker-Fletcher, Karen *Dancing with God: Trinity in a Womanist Perspective* (St. Louis: Chalice Press, 2006).

—, Sisters of Dust, *Sisters of Spirit: Womanist Wordings of Creation* (Minneapolis: Fortress Press, 1995).

Baltazar, Eulalio *The Dark Center: A Process Theology of Blackness* (New York: Paulist Press, 1973).

Barbour, Ian *Religion in an Age of Science* (New York: Harper San Francisco, 1990).

Beardslee, William *A House for Hope: A Study in Process and Biblical Thought* (Philadelphia: Westminster Press, 1972).

Birch, Charles and John Cobb, *The Liberation of Life: From Cell to Community* (Denton, TX: Environmental Ethics Books, 1990).

Bowman, Donna *The Divine Decision: A Process Doctrine of Election* (Louisville: Westminster/John Knox Press, 2002).

Bracken, Joseph and Marjorie Suchocki, eds., *Trinity in Process: A Relational Theology of God* (New York: Continuum, 1997).

Brock, Rita Nakashima *Journeys by Heart: A Christology of Erotic Power* (New York: Crossroad, 1988).

Brock, Rita Nakashima and Rebecca Ann Parker, *Proverbs of Ashes: Violence, Redemptive Suffering and the Search for What Saves Us* (Boston: Beacon Press, 1992).

—, *Saving Paradise: How Christianity Traded the Love of This World for Crucifixion and Empire* (Boston: Beacon Press, 2009).

Brown, Delwin *To Set at Liberty: Christian Faith and Human Freedom* (Maryknoll, NY: Orbis, 1981).

Clayton, Philip *Adventures in the Spirit* (Minneapolis: Fortress Press, 2008).

—, *Transforming Christian Theology* (Minneapolis: Fortress Press, 1999).

Cobb, John B. *A Christian Natural Theology: Based on the Thought of Alfred North Whitehead* (Philadelphia: Westminster Press, 1965).

—, *Becoming a Thinking Christian* (Nashville: Abingdon, 1993).

—, *Beyond Dialogue: Toward a Mutual Transformation of Buddhism and Christianity* (Philadelphia: Fortress Press, 1982).

—, *Can Christ Become Good News Again?* (St. Louis: Chalice Press, 1991).

—, *Christ in a Pluralistic Age* (Philadelphia: Westminster Press, 1975).

—, *Doubting Thomas: Christology in Story Form* (New York: Crossroads, 1990).

—, *God and the World* (Philadelphia: Westminster Press, 1969).

—, *Grace and Responsibility: A Wesleyan Theology for Today* (Nashville: Abingdon Press, 1995).

—, *Lay Theology* (St. Louis: Chalice, 1991).

—, *Matters of Life and Death* (Nashville: Westminster/John Knox, 1991).

—, *Praying for Jennifer: An Exploration of Intercessory Prayer in Story Form* (Upper Room, 1985).

—, *Process Theology as Political Theology* (Philadelphia: Westminster/John Knox, 1982).

—, *Reclaiming the Church: Where the Mainline Church Went Wrong and What it Can Do About It* (Nashville: Westminster/John Knox, 1997).

—, *The Structure of Christian Existence* (Philadelphia: Westminster Press, 1969).

—, *Whitehead Word Book* (Claremont, CA: P&F Press, 2008).

Cobb, John B. and Herman Daly, *For the Common Good: Redirecting the Economy Toward Community, the Environment, and a Sustainable Future* (Boston: Beacon Press, 1989).

Cobb, John B. and David Ray Griffin, *Process Theology: An Introductory Exposition* (Philadelphia: Westminster Press, 1976).

Cobb, John B. and Clark Pinnock, eds., *Searching for an Adequate God: A Dialogue between Process and Free-will Theists* (Grand Rapids: Wm. B. Eerdmans, 2000).

Coleman, Monica *Making a Way Out of Now Way: A Womanist Theology* (Minneapolis: Fortress Press, 2008).

Cousins, Ewart *Process Theology: Basic Writings* (New York: Newman Press, 1971).

Epperly, Bruce *At the Edges of Life: Death and the Human Adventure* (St. Louis: Chalice Press, 1992).

—, *God's Touch: Faith, Wholeness, and Healing Miracles of Jesus* (Louisville: Westminster/John Knox, 2001).

—, *Healing Worship: Purpose and Practice* (Cleveland: Pilgrim Press, 2006).

—, *Holy Adventure: Forty-one Days of Audacious Living* (Nashville: Upper Room Books, 2008).

—, *Tending to the Holy* (Herndon, VA: Alban Institute, 2009), written with Katherine Gould Epperly.

Epperly, Bruce, John Cobb, and Paul Nancarrow, *The Call of the Spirit: Process Theology in a Relational World* (Claremont, CA: P&F Press, 2005).

Faber, Roland *God as Poet of the World: Exploring Process Theologies* (Philadelphia: Westminster/John Knox, 2008).

Farmer, Patricia *Embracing a Beautiful God* (St. Louis: Chalice Press, 2003).

—, *The Metaphor Maker* (Scots Valley: Estrella de Mar Publications, 2009).

Farmer, Ronald *Awakening.* (Scots Valley: Create Space, 2009).

—, *Beyond the Impasse: The Promise of a Process Hermeneutic* (Macon, GA: Mercer University Press, 1997).

Ford, Lewis *The Lure of God: A Biblical Background for Process Theism* (Philadelphia: Westminster Press, 1978).

Fretheim, Terence *The Suffering God* (Philadelphia: Fortress Press, 1984).

Gnuse, Robert *The Old Testament and Process Theology* (St. Louis: Chalice Press, 2000).

Griffin, David Ray *God, Power, and Evil: A Process Theodicy* (Philadelphia: Westminster Press, 1976).

—, *God and Religion in the Post-modern World: Essays in Post-modern Theology* (New York: State University of New York Press, 1989).

—, *Parapsychology, Philosophy, and Spirituality: A Postmodern Exploration* (Albany: State University of New York Press, 1997).

—, *A Process Christology* (Philadelphia: Westminster, 1973).

—, *Reenchantment without Supernaturalism: A Process Theology of Religion* (Ithaca: Cornell University Press, 2001).

—, *The Reenchantment of Science: Postmodern Proposals* (Albany: State University of New York Press, 1988).

Hartshorne, Charles *Anselm's Discovery: A Re-examination of the Ontological Proof of God* (LaSalle, IL: Open Court, 1965).

—, *Creative Synthesis and Philosophic Method* (New York: University Press of America, 1983).

—, *The Divine Relativity: A Social Conception of God* (New Haven, CT: Yale University Press, 1948).

—, *Omnipotence and Other Theological Mistakes* (Albany: State University of New York Press, 1984).

—, *Reality as Social Process* (New York: Free Press, 1953).

—, *Whitehead's Philosophy* (Lincoln: University of Nebraska Press, 1972).

John Haught, *Cosmic Adventure: Science, Religion, and the Quest for Purpose,* (Mahwah, NJ: Paulist Press, 1995).

Kaufman, William *The Case for God* (St. Louis: Chalice Press, 1991).

Keller, Catherine *Apocalypse Now and Then: A Feminist Guide to the End of the World* (Boston: Beacon Press, 1996).

—, *The Face of the Deep: A Theology of Becoming* (New York: Routledge, 2003).

—, *From a Broken Web: Separation, Sexism, and Self* (Boston: Beacon Press, 1986).

—, *On the Mystery: Discerning God in Process* (Minneapolis: Fortress Press, 2008).

Lowe, Victor *Alfred North Whitehead: The Man and His Work,* volume 1, 1861–1910 (Baltimore: Johns Hopkins University Press, 1985).

—, *Alfred North Whitehead: The Man and His Work,* volume 2, 1910–1947 (Baltimore: Johns Hopkins Press, 1990).

Lubarsky, Sandra *Tolerance and Transformation: Jewish Approaches to Religious Pluralism* (Cincinnati: Hebrew Union College Press, 1990).

McDaniel, Jay *Gandhi's Truth: Learning from the World's Religions as a Path to Peace* (New York: Orbis, 2005).

—, *Living from the Center: Spirituality in an Age of Consumerism* (St. Louis: Chalice, 2000)

—, *Of God and Pelicans: A Theology of Reverence for Life* (Louisville: Westminster/John Knox, 1998).

—, *What is Process Thought? Seven Answers to Seven Questions* (Claremont: P&F Press, 2008).

—, *With Roots and Wings: Christianity in an Age of Ecology and Dialogue* (Eugene, OR: Wipf and Stock, 2009).

McDaniel, Jay and Donna Bowman, *A Handbook of Process Theology* (St. Louis: Chalice Press, 2006).

Meland, Bernard *Fallible Forms and Symbols* (Philadelphia: Fortress Press, 1976).

Mellert, Robert *What is Process Theology? An Introduction to the Philosophy of Alfred North Whitehead and How It Is Being Applied to Christian Thought Today* (New York: Paulist Press, 1975).

Mesle, C. Robert *Process-Relational Philosophy: An Introduction to Alfred North Whitehead* (West Conshohocken, PA: Templeton Foundation Press, 2008).

—, *Process Theology: A Basic Introduction* (St. Louis: Chalice, 1993).

Neville, Robert *Creativity and God: A Challenge to Process Theology* (Albany: State University of New York Press, 1995).

Ogden, Schubert *Faith and Freedom* (Nashville: Abingdon Press, 1989).

—, *The Reality of God and Other Essays* (New York: Harper and Row, 1991).

Oord, Thomas Jay *The Nature of Love: A Theology* (St. Louis: Chalice Press, 2010).

Peters, Eugene *The Creative Advance: An Introduction to Process Theology as the Context for Faith* (St. Louis: Bethany Press, 1966).

Pittenger, W. Norman, *The Divine Triunity* (New York: United Church Press, 1977).

—, *God's Way with Men* (New York: Hodder and Stoughton, 1966).

—, *The Holy Spirit* (New York: United Church Press, 1974).

—, *The Word Incarnate: A Study of the Doctrine of the Person of Christ* (New York: Harper and Row, 1959).

—, *Time for Consent: A Christian's Approach to Homosexuality* (London: SCM, 1996).

Polkinghorne, John *Quarks, Chaos, and Creation* (New York: Crossroads, 1998).

—, *Traffic in Truth: Exchanges Between Science and Theology* (Minneapolis: Fortress Press, 2000).

Pregeant, Russell *Christology Beyond Dogma: Matthew's Christ in Process Hermeneutic* (Philadelphia: Fortress Press, 1978).

Price, Lucien *The Dialogues of Alfred North Whitehead* (Boston: Little Brown and Company, 1954).

Russell, Helene Tallon *Iragaray and Kierkegaard: On the Construction of the Self* (Macon, GA: Mercer University Press, 2009).

Sturm, Douglas ed., *Belonging Together: Faith and Politics in a Relational World* (Claremont: P&F Press, 2003).

Sturm, Douglas *Community and Alienation: Essays on Process Thought and Public Life* (South Bend, Indiana: University of Notre Dame Press, 1988).
—, *Solidarity and Suffering: Towards a Politics of Relationality* (Albany: State University of New York Press, 1998).
Suchocki, Marjorie *Diversity and Divinity: A Christian Affirmation of Religious Pluralism* (Nashville: Abingdon Press, 2003).
—, *The End of Evil: Process Eschatology in Historical Context* (Albany: State University of New York Press, 1988).
—, *The Fall to Violence: Original Sin in Relational Theology* (New York: Continuum, 1995).
—, *God, Christ, Church: A Practical Guide to Process Theology* (New York: Crossroad, 1982).
—, *In God's Presence: Theological Reflections on Prayer* (St. Louis: Chalice Press, 1996).
—, *The Whispered Word* (St. Louis: Chalice Press, 1999).
Whitehead, Alfred North *Adventures of Ideas* (New York: Free Press, 1967)
—, *Modes of Thought* (New York: Free Press, 1968).
—, *Process and Reality: Corrected Edition.* Edited by David Ray Griffin and Donald Sherburne (New York: Free Press, 1978).
—, *Religion in the Making* (New York: Meridian, 1960).
—, *Science and the Modern Word* (New York: Free Press, 1967).
—, *The Function of Reason* (Boston: Beacon Press, 1971).
Wieman, Henry Nelson *The Source of Human Good* (Carbondale: Southern Illinois University Press, 1946).
Williams, Daniel Day *The Spirit and the Forms of Love* (New York: Harper and Row, 1968).
Williamson, Clark *A Guest in the House of Israel: Post-Holocaust Church Theology* (Louisville: Westminster/John Knox, 1993).
—, *Way of Blessing, Way of Life: A Theology* (St. Louis: Chalice, 1999).
Young, Henry James *Hope in Process: A Theology of Social Pluralism* (Minneapolis: Fortress Press, 1990).

INDEX